THE WIVES OF LOS ALAMOS

Their average age was twenty-five. They came from all over the States, and arrived in New Mexico ready for adventure — or, at least, resigned to it. But hope quickly turned to hardship in the desolate military town where everything was a secret; including what their husbands were doing at the lab . . . They were constrained by the words they couldn't say, the letters they couldn't send, the freedom they didn't have. Though they were strangers, they joined together: babies were born, friendships were forged, and children grew up. But then 'the project' was unleashed, and even bigger challenges faced the women of Los Alamos as they struggled with the burden of their contribution towards the most destructive force in human history: the atomic bomb.

TARASHEA NESBIT

THE WIVES OF LOS ALAMOS

Complete and Unabridged

ULVERSCROFT
Leicester

First published in Great Britain in 2014 by
Bloomsbury Publishing plc
London

First Large Print Edition
published 2015
by arrangement with
Bloomsbury Publishing plc
London

A catalogue record for this book is available
from the British Library.

ISBN 978–1–4448–2436–0

Published by
F. A. Thorpe (Publishing)
Anstey, Leicestershire

Set by Words & Graphics Ltd.
Anstey, Leicestershire
Printed and bound in Great Britain by
T. J. International Ltd., Padstow, Cornwall

This book is printed on acid-free paper

For Jerritt.

For Margot.

1943

WEST

Over the Black Sea, the Mediterranean, the Pacific, the Arctic, the Atlantic; in sewers, in trenches, on the ocean, in the sky: there was a war going on. Sometimes it seemed far away, barely happening, but then a mother or a wife placed a gold star in her living room window — her brother, her husband, her son, our neighbor — and the war became personal.

It was March, gas was rationed; therefore the streets were quiet. We heard a car pull up in the driveway. We wiped our hands on our apron and placed the apron on the dishes. The doorbell rang and a young man, just slightly older than our husbands, about thirty-five, stood on our porch in a porkpie hat and asked whether the professor was home. His eyes were the color of stillness — something between a pale body of water and the fog that emerges above it. Although dinner was almost ready our house was chilly — we could not turn on the gas heater — and we invited him in but felt embarrassed by the cold. Our husbands came downstairs and they shook hands. This man was tall, but his shoulders stooped as if he had spent his life trying to appear smaller than he was in order to make others comfortable.

He asked our husbands about their research at the university, we asked him to stay for dinner; he declined but said to our husbands, *I've got a proposal*, and together they walked down the hallway to our husband's office, and the door closed behind them.

When they came out an hour later our husbands were flushed and smiling. They shook the man's hand, smiled, and walked him out.

Our husbands joined us in the kitchen and said, *We are going to the desert*, and we had no choice except to say *Oh my!* as if this sounded like great fun. *Where?* we asked, and no one answered. If we were the ones to see the man to the door — the future Director of our future unknown location — on the front porch he said to us, *I think you will like life up there.* We asked, *Where is 'up there' exactly?* He hesitated and said, *My two loves are physics and the desert. My wife is my mistress*, and winked at us. We watched him walk down the sidewalk two blocks and turn the corner.

Or it did not happen like that at all. One day, after we read books to our children, after we folded their blankets back, kissed them, tried to hurry along their sleep, we came downstairs to find our husbands smoking a pipe in their wingback chair, the orange one, an ugly thing we did not like, and we heard them ask us, *How'd you like to live in the Southwest?* and we plopped down on the couch, and we bounced the seat cushions, just as our children did, which annoyed us, although, when we did it, we found it exceedingly enjoyable. We were European women born in Southampton and Hamburg, Western women born in California and Montana, East Coast women born in Connecticut and New York, Midwestern women born in Nebraska and Ohio, or Southern women from Mississippi or Texas, and no matter who we were we wanted nothing to do with starting all over again, and so we paused, we exhaled, and we asked, *What part of the Southwest?*

Our husbands muttered, *I don't know.* And we thought that was strange.

Or one winter day our husbands came home with burns on their right arms and told us their bosses said they needed to go west to recuperate. Out west there would be work, they said, though they could not give any more specifics about where *out west.*

We had degrees from Mount Holyoke, as our grandmothers did, or from a junior college, as our fathers insisted. We had doctorates from Yale; we had coursework from MIT and Cornell: we were certain we could discover for ourselves just where we would be moving. What did we know about the Southwest? A new dam, Hoover, that could, perhaps, power a grand experiment in the desert. To this and other conjectures we asked our husbands to nod *Yes* or *No. You won't be telling,* we said. But no matter how seductively or how kindly we asked *Where?* and placed a hand on their chest, our husbands would not say, even if they did know, which we suspected they did.

A few of us of us had experienced secrecy already. Our husbands were professors at Columbia or the University of Chicago and just that past month the Physics Lab was renamed the Metallurgical Lab, though no one in the lab, especially our husbands, were metallurgists, or did any kind of metal extracting. The college hired armed guards to be posted inside the doors of the Metallurgical Lab, and in the last weeks even the wives were no longer permitted to enter.

Our husbands said, *I'll go on ahead*, or, *We'll all go together*, or, *I can't say when I will arrive but you should get on the train and set up house now*. We suggested our husbands take a job in Canada instead. They declined the suggestion. And if they told us we were going to the Southwest, perhaps saying, *We are going away and that's the end of the discussion*, we went to the university library and found the only three travel books about the Southwest. And the card in the back pocket of the New Mexico book had the names of our husbands' colleagues who disappeared weeks before *to some strange wilderness*, people had said. We knew then that New Mexico was probably where we were going, too. We felt we had partially solved the mystery.

If our husbands told us, *We are going away and that's the end of the discussion*, we knew not to ask another thing, and we kept our partially solved mysteries to ourselves.

Those of us with husbands who were going to have *manager* in their titles got to know, immediately, the general location of our future home. Our husbands informed us we were going to Site Y, outside Santa Fe. We wrote a list of things we wanted to know about our new town for our husbands to ask *them* about

— we did not know who *they* and *them* were. We typed: *How are the schools? Is there a hospital? Is there adequate help? What size are the windows? How is the weather?*

Replies came back from our husbands over dinner as they passed the Brussels sprouts. They told us, *Rest assured, your children will receive the finest education.* And, *The hospital will take care of all your needs.* And, *You will be provided with excellent cleaning and childcare help. The roads can get muddy — bring your rubbers!* We raised our eyebrows. It sounded funny, official, and suspect, but we said, *That sounds nice.* We were not told that the school, the homes, and the hospital had not yet been built.

A week before we left, a gentleman came to the door, showed us a badge, and said, *Do you mind if I ask you a few questions?* Over iced tea and stale sugar cookies we were quizzed about our presence at a Marxist Pedagogy meeting in 1940, or we were asked why we were on the list of members of the League of Women Shoppers, and didn't we know that that organization was a Communist front? We were only a year out of Russia and was it true we had been captains in the Russian Army? Was it true we taught English

8

classes for the Communist Party worker's school in Youngstown, Ohio?

It was likely our husbands were questioned as well, though many were less interested in discussing the interrogation. We told the short man with the inscrutable expressions that we wanted nothing to do with the Communist Party, that we were never involved, or that we weren't involved anymore. We said we had only been associated with them because of a previous love affair, and we did not see the point anymore, or we had become disillusioned after Pearl Harbor. We were asked to name our affiliates, and we said it was difficult to recall the people we knew then, that our memory was fuzzy on the dates and locations. We said this even if our memory was not fuzzy. We did not want to get anyone in trouble. Judging by his scowling face, this man did not like these answers. However, he went away, and no one else came to see us, and so it seemed we were still leaving for the wilderness.

Some of our husbands left first. We watched them disappear into train terminals, through the doors of unmarked black sedans, down airport runways, and we were left behind, overwhelmed. We called our friends from the phone booth and they met us at the train station or at our house with a loaf of bread, or a chicken casserole and a flask. We wondered aloud how we would ever survive without our friends to comfort us. We wanted to tell them everything we knew and everything we worried about — how scared we were and how excited. We wanted to ask their advice about what to bring to the Southwest — dresses, shoes, lotions — but we could not.

On our last day we went to see *Oklahoma!* on Broadway or *For Whom the Bell Tolls* at the Mayan Theatre and we ate at the Italian restaurant, Luciano's, that we had always wanted to try. We returned our library books, we picked up a copy of the family medical records, we took a long walk alone and asked ourselves why we had not done this sooner. We saw, for what seemed like the first time, the things we liked about the city we were leaving — whispering to the other wives at the community swimming pool, seeing women our mothers' ages leaning in close to one another at the teahouse. And though we never actually went to the teahouse we found ourselves smiling every time we walked by it. We thought we would be joyful saying good-bye to the unfriendly pharmacist, Mr. Williams, but that was not true.

We took the car to the shop to get the oil changed. We dropped off our children's old bike tires, our worn-out bathing cap, and a bucket of nails our husbands left in the garage at the Junior League's Metal and Rubber Drive. We bought a few more war bonds. Some of us had been smart enough to ask about gas and electric, and on our last day we bought an electric toaster, because we were told that where we were going would not have natural gas. We went to the ration office and handed a sealed envelope to the woman at the counter, as our husbands had instructed. She read the letter inside, gave us a curious look, and provided us with enough gas rations to get our car to the other side of the country.

We went to Barbara's and got a manicure; we requested a bright cherry red, even though we knew it would chip by the end of the day. We sewed curtains for rooms we had never seen, hoping the colors would look right and the dimensions would be correct. We packed the linens and not the piano, and we were secretly happy to realize our children would not be able to continue lessons where we were going — we were told there was no piano teacher — which meant we would no longer have to hear them practicing *Chopsticks* over and over again.

Or we were appalled our children would not have the necessary experience of piano at a young age and though we did not think we made good teachers — we were too soft, or we were too impatient — once we arrived and unpacked our dishes, we volunteered to teach piano in the lodge, which was also the movie theater, the gymnasium, and the community mess hall. Several children would learn to play Bach after dinner.

We lied and told our children we were packing because we would be spending August with their grandparents in Denver or Duluth. Or we said we did not know where we were going, which was the truth, but our children, who did not trust that adults went places without knowing where they were going, thought we were lying. Or we told them it was an adventure and they would find out when we got there.

The movers came and out went our sofa, our books, and our cutlery. As they loaded boxes, our neighbors drove past, slowed down, doubled back, and asked, *Where you headed?*, and, *Why didn't you tell us? We would have thrown you a party*, and, *You've been great neighbors. You'll be missed.* We said, *Vacation*, or, *Change of scenery*, or, *Jim's work.*

Our neighbors did not believe us, though they smiled as if they did.

We boarded trains in Philadelphia, or in Chicago, with GIs all looking identical in their dog tags, their black-rimmed glasses, their gosling-short hair. Perhaps it was unpatriotic, but we were annoyed at the GIs who ate before us and delayed our dinners until ten o'clock, and who therefore made our children less manageable. Though we were only twenty-five, we were tired, and we were with our children, who reminded us of what we were tethered to, children who were bored for hours and who pinched and kicked one another. When our children whined, *He hit me! She started it!* after eight hours on the train we ran out of ways to keep them occupied, and instead we finally just stared out the window as if we were noticing the beige nuances of tan landscapes, which we were not. By the time we arrived we had seen so many mountains they had lost any sense of the majestic.

Or, less frequently, our husbands went with us. They drove us in red Studebakers, in green Oldsmobiles, our backseats filled with clothes, books, children, and the family cat, Roscoe, who meowed for hours. We stopped along the way to visit our parents, who asked repeatedly where we were going, and whom we could not tell.

Our fathers pounded their fists on the table, said, *You think we are Nazi spies? Tell us!* Our mothers said, *Be careful.* Or, *Write me as soon as you can.* And our children got fearful, and cried, *Tell them*, but we did not tell them, or our children. Later, when our fathers cooled off, when they said, touching our arm, *I'm your father, you can tell me anything*, we did not tell them where we were going, because we still did not know.

We hugged our mothers, pecked our fathers on the cheek, glanced out the window to see our husbands checking the air pressure in the tires. Our mothers understood; our mothers had kept great secrets. We loaded up the children, the cat, and the snacks, and headed west.

US

We were round-faced, athletic, boisterous, austere, thin-boned, catlike, and awkward. When we challenged people's political views we were described as stubborn or outspoken. Our fathers were academics — we knew the academic world. We married men just like our fathers, or nothing like them, or only the best parts. As the wives of scientists in college towns we gave tea parties and gossiped, or we lived in the city and hosted cocktail hours. We served cigarettes on tin trays. We leaned in close to the other wives, pretending we were good friends, cupping our hands and whispering into their ears. And, most importantly, we found out how to get our husbands tenure.

Not all of us were born in America and not all of us knew the academic world. Some of our parents had immigrated while our own mothers were in their third trimester with us, and some of us had immigrated when we were newly married and not yet pregnant ourselves. We left Paris when we heard the Germans were taking over the city, or we left

Italy when we woke one cold January morning to hear a Nazi anthem being sung in an upbeat tenor outside our bedroom window. We asked, *What is happening to the world?* We packed two suitcases. Our husbands told the military men at the checkpoint we were just leaving on holiday, and we boarded a plane to America instead.

Some of us remembered World War I from the vantage point of elementary school age worries — going without salt, butter, and cookies — and now as young adults we did not want to get involved.

Or we thought about the December morning in 1941 when the Japanese — depending on who told the story — were angered by trade embargoes that restricted their purchase of oil and metals, or wanted to possess all of the islands in the Pacific Ocean. We went to Spanish Relief parties the night before Pearl Harbor with our husbands, and the next day, when the war broke out, we both decided there were more pressing crises than the Spanish cause. That was three years ago, and we had followed so much news it was hard to keep up. But we knew this: Germany's Hitler and Italy's Mussolini were taking over Europe. Japan's Tojo was dominating the

Pacific. We heard Japan was getting closer to their goal — they had captured Borneo, Java, and Sumatra, they had overthrown the British-ruled Singapore — and in Europe the news of German occupations gave many of us the desire to do *something*. The Axis and the Allies. *Would it never end?*

We arrived in New Mexico and thought we had come to the end of the earth, or we thought we had come home. It was ninety-four degrees and the sun was merciless, even in the early evening. We traveled up, up, up, along switchbacks, passing the flat tops of the mesas and, as seen from high enough, their fingerlike cliffs. Down below, the Rio Grande picked up soil on the banks and made a deep red river for as far as we could see. We saw the pink flowering cholla, the red-orange flowers of the claret cup cactus, the yellow blossoms of the prickly pear. We drove through the guts of mountains — brown, yellow, pink, and gray strata stretching sky-high — cut away to make this road and cut away by centuries of water and wind.

We stepped off trains nine months pregnant, or carrying six-week-olds in clothes baskets, or holding the hands of our two-year-olds

— our Bobbys and our Margarets. Our Marcias got chicken pox along the way and were quarantined to the back of the train. We arrived at 7,200 feet above sea level dizzy, sweaty, and nauseous. We arrived short of breath in high heels, green silk blouses that tied at the collar, and blue skirts — our best outfits — damp, wrinkled, and clinging to our backs. We arrived in need of a shampoo. In gloves, in hats; as if we had never left the city. As if the sand and dirt and dust were not in our hair, in our teeth. As if we were not resentful that we did not have a choice.

We got off at Lamy, looked around, and saw no one except a handsome woman in blue jeans. She was tall, so tall, slender, and had a police dog at her side. So this was New Mexico.

Or we were told to transfer from the train in Lamy to a bus and once we got off in Santa Fe someone would be there looking for us. No one was there waiting, and we arrived teary and red-eyed and peered into the glass case of pecan pies at the diner in Santa Fe, the only thing open and decent at that hour — five A.M., eleven P.M. — until a waitress in a starched cotton dress looked us up and down and said, *Ma'am, you're looking for 109 East Palace. Around the corner.*

18

Or we arrived looking for the office and entered a bakery and we thought there must be a trick, that we must order a loaf of bread for access to the secret location, but we stumbled on our order because we were not given instructions on what exactly to ask for. So we said things in a tone punctuated with question marks, often requesting items that were not on the menu — *Pain au chocolat?* or *Bagel?* The bored baker interrupted, *You must be looking for the office down the way. Take a left.* We thanked him. We took a left.

We went around the corner, followed the sidewalk, and passed adobe houses, houses built with the soil surrounding them. We passed the curved corners of walls smoothed by numerous hands and houses hanging with tricolored corn and chiles. Our children asked, *Where are we?*

Nailed to a white door was a metal sign, *109.* Our children ran toward it, opening the screen door, which banged loudly behind us. A woman in pearls, in a pink or blue tweed suit, with an upturned nose, held two black telephone receivers to both ears and said, inaudibly, just mouthed, *I'll be right with you.* A small white dog rested at her feet and opened one eye to look at us. The woman had friendly, bulbous cheeks, and when she put the receivers back on the cradles she went over the specific rules of our new home. We thought she must have encountered several like us before — tired, weary, expectant, nervous — which was true, she had.

Dorothy took our pictures, our fingerprints, and informed us we would be getting a new name. Some of us had been told this would happen, others were shocked, and a few were simply resigned. Though many of our husbands were celebrities among academic and physics circles, the point here, in our new home, was not to draw attention. And so, despite our thick Italian or Danish accents that would give our heritage away as soon as we spoke, we became something more all-American: *Mrs. Fermi* became *Mrs. Farmer* and *Mrs. Mueller* was now *Mrs. Miller.* We knew that we were becoming part of an entity larger than our families, larger than ourselves, and we were not necessarily happy about it. Our husbands were not around to hear our complaints, or if they were around we felt we could not bother them with our petty grievances. Our son Bill, who was almost ten, who was looking forward to the desert, announced, when the tips of our fingers were dark with ink, *We are important!* This was the first (though not last) time our sons exclaimed this.

Come by if you need anything, Dorothy said. She gave us a yellow map that marked every mile from where we were to where we were going with red pencil, all the way to our final destination, called the Hill, which was thirty-five more miles, all up. We would not have a phone. We did not have a car. How could we possibly come by if we needed anything?

Our husbands' friends met us with a borrowed Army car and drove us the thirty-five miles uphill. Or we got on an Army bus parked outside 109 East Palace, a large machine that released thick gray clouds of exhaust. A man tipped his hat and loaded the bus with our mops, brooms, and potted plants. We looked around to see several other tense faces, but none that were familiar. We smiled and took off our gloves. We wondered which of them would become our friends, or we decided immediately whom we thought we would like to be friends with.

And if we were with our husbands, at Otowi we took a one-lane suspension bridge that was so rickety only small cars could use it.

Our bodies swayed as we rounded sharp corners and our husbands sang *People Will Say We're in Love* and for a moment this unknown future could be an adventure, could be almost romantic. We turned on the radio because we were too curious not to, and thankfully instead of bad news we heard that the U.S. and British forces had landed in Sicily. We felt light with hope. High up on a mountain we saw a spiral of spinning dust.

Miles later we were the ones driving. We took a bend too quickly. Our children yelled, *Stop!* As the car slowed they flung the doors open and vomited in the middle of the gravel road.

We arrived newlyweds, or with a seven-year itch, or still great friends, or no longer in love but trying to keep it together for our children, or for ourselves. Some of us always expected disaster and kept the shades drawn low, some of us were quietly skeptical, although no one could tell, and we were nicknamed Polly. Some of us always made do and we quickly established knitting circles and book clubs. Some of us thrived on gatherings, and we created dance nights and afternoon teas and bridge clubs. Though the dance parties of the night before still lingered, we were Catholic and had Sunday service in Fuller Lodge at eight

A.M., or we were Protestant and had service at ten A.M. As we walked into the lodge we smelled dank, cheap beer, and the spilled drinks made our shoes catch on the sticky wood floor.

Like many moving toward an unknown future, we clung to the beliefs that had carried us this far — about people, the world, our husbands, the war — until that strategy could no longer assuage our fears.

UNTIL WE FOUND OUR OWN

The bus stopped at a barbed wire fence, and a man in a deep green uniform and a large gun at his hip stood tall at the gate. We had been told by our husbands to be careful what we said, but when the man boarded the bus and asked us for our identification, when the man in uniform said, *Mrs. Miller,* and we forgot our fake name for a moment, or we were not sure if we were supposed to tell him the truth, our real name, we corrected him: *Mrs. Mueller, you mean,* and he lowered his eyebrows and moved in close to us, and we smelled coffee, or vodka, or onions, and he replied, *No. You are Mrs. Miller now.* It was not until then that we realized the gravity of what our husbands meant when they told us to be careful. We were no longer in charge of ourselves or even our own names.

At the fence was a sign: *U.S. Government property. Danger! Peligro! Keep out.* Down below we saw Dobermans patrolling the bases of the cliffs, and above, on the peaks, we saw men on horseback standing lookout. In front of us, a six-foot rattlesnake hung on the guard gate. If it was night the military police officers shined flashlights into our cars and into our children's sleeping eyes; and if it was day they asked us to step out of the vehicle.

Some of us were not yet U.S. citizens; we were from the enemy's country, Germany, but we were not the enemy, and the Director vouched for us. Or we arrived and our passes were not ready and it was night and the Director was not available, and we could hear the coyotes echoing down the canyon. We were told to stay in the car until morning, and although it was summer the night was cold. We were pregnant. We do not remember how much we slept, but it felt like little, until finally, finally, the sun rose over the Sangre de Cristo Mountains. Someone official woke up and walked toward us and apologized and confirmed that we were who they said we were. We handed over our cameras. We denied we kept a diary. We received our clearances and continued through the gate, up the muddy unpaved road, past plots of land piled with felled trees and drywall and tubs of paint, past cranes and bulldozers, past a fast-moving truck, until we arrived at rows and rows of identical houses, until we found our own.

Or we arrived without our husbands and we were greeted by Donald *Moll* Flanders in the Housing Office who ordered someone named Bob to show us to our home and take us to the square dance that evening. And when our husbands did arrive they came with a bodyguard. We were amazed: *Our husbands needed a bodyguard?*

Since we had no children, or because we arrived later than the others, we were assigned not to a house but to an apartment on the second floor. It was stuffy inside but we could not open the windows because they were painted shut. We were disappointed or angry but when we entered our apartment we found a vase of wildflowers on the kitchen counter, a pitcher of milk in the icebox, and a note: *Welcome to the neighborhood! — Katherine & Louise.*

Or we arrived and stepped out of the car and Ingrid was already walking out of her door toward us, and she said her name and tried to give us half her teaching shift. We arrived and Erica was in the next yard over saying soothing words in Swiss German to her daughter who was on the ground with muddy knees, crying, and Starla called out to those of us within shouting distance: *I just saved these trees from the military!* and pointed to the three pines in her front yard. Louise opened her front door and exclaimed, *The Allies reclaimed Sicily!* The two agreed it was high time to celebrate, and called a tea party — or was it a cocktail hour? — for three o'clock.

Or we arrived as the first wall of our house was being nailed, and we wept. The week before we left we ordered from Marshall Field everything a new wife might need, but we arrived and were told, *Your boxes won't be here until next month*, and we did not even have a pot, a spoon, or a dish. So we made fast friends with the Mormon family next door and for two months we ate off their floral-patterned plates instead of our own.

If it was night when we first arrived, we got out of the car and walked forward, our feet, still in high heels, were pricked by the gravel. Our husbands led the way with a light. We walked toward our number written on a yellow piece of paper given to us in Santa Fe — our four, our number ten. It was a slanted piece of land and a piñon pine without a structure to sleep in.

Our husbands led the way with a light, except they did not know exactly where our new home was situated, and so we moved forward and then retraced our steps. Someone called to us in the distance. The voice got closer and a man appeared, he was tall, and he said, *Very sorry, we were expecting you later, it's not ready yet, come to the lodge.* We were cold, but we smiled even though it hurt our cheeks to smile, and we went into the lodge and made our way to our sleeping bags on the floor.

Though we did not know it then, this was something men, women, and children across the West were also doing, in former horse stables swept out but still smelling, on gymnasium floors with a hundred others, with their one allowable suitcase, with a four-digit number pinned to the collar of their coats. We were white, or we passed for white, or we were not white, but we did not look Japanese, and we thought they went to a place where they could be protected from other Americans who might hate them because they were from enemy country. Because we did not know they would be net makers and would be *protected* by men who had lost their legs in the Pacific theater, what we felt was for ourselves, a bit of pity, and for our children, a bit of fear, and for our husbands, a bit of anger, and we undressed, and we tried to sleep.

We told our children, *This is an adventure!* though we preferred the adventure of something new and exciting with the potential for a high return — a love affair, say — rather than a risky undertaking with a probably unfavorable outcome, like the Klondike gold rush. Our husbands saw our faces and said, *You'll love the country once you get used to it.*

We tried to sleep but we could not. We thought about our mothers who, when we got married, said, *Marriage is not easy.* We thought about our mothers who said, *He is a good man,* and our mothers who said, *Be kind to him.* Our mothers who said the secret to a good marriage was a clean house and a warm meal, our mothers who said the secret was keeping quiet, or our mothers who said the secret to a good marriage was picking your battles. Or, for one of our mothers, the secret to a good marriage, she said, was sex.

We thought of our mothers who were right now on the back porch enjoying a cigarette, our mothers who were standing in the kitchen wrapping up a plate in tinfoil and putting it in the oven to keep warm, we thought of our mothers writing letters to our brothers who were crossing oceans we would never see. We

29

thought of our mothers who were drinking gin gimlets with our fathers, who were dancing with our fathers at a party, who were drawing a bath, who were asleep. Our mothers who told us they were so proud of us. We thought of our mothers and we knew this was not our home, this New Mexico. Nevertheless, we would make the best of it.

LAND

In the morning we saw the view we had of the Sangre de Cristo Mountains to the east, the range jagged like shark's teeth. And close behind us, we saw the green tops of the Jemez Mountains. The land was built up from eruptions and worn down by erosions. The Jemez volcano made a vast, flat meadow surrounded by rocky cliffs and in most seasons, when the wind brushed over the meadow, it became a rolling wave of grasses.

We called what we lived on — on the other side of the Jemez rim — a mesa, because we recognized the image from our college textbooks, or we called it a mesa because someone told us that was what it was. But it was not a mesa, exactly; it was a *potrero*, a dry tongue of land. The shaggy forest gave way to sudden cliffs and we could see we were isolated on three sides, like a high fortress with a deep moat. To mostly everything out there, we did not exist. The light shimmered and stretched our own views. And in the eastern side of the sky we saw the alpenglow, a bright red band on the horizon, as if the sun were setting in both the west and the east, and we did not think about the optics; we just thought it was beautiful.

The sparse landscape felt isolating and disturbing. Or to see so much with so little in it was relaxing, and we admired the quiet. Some of us could understand why, before us, people from big cities visited here to regain their strength in the fresh dry air.

We squinted and wrapped a scarf over our foreheads. Some of us did not burn easily but many of us did. We came from sunny places and we thought the light was bright and cheerful or we came from overcast places and saw the light as harsh and comfortless.

Our houses, cars, and skin appeared covered by another skin, a skin not our own but the sandy, warm-toned skin of the desert. The spring rain created a carpet of yellow and purple wildflowers we could see in the distant desert meadow. And after the rain, the sagebrush filled the air with a smell like camphor — sweet, but medicinal. Rainstorms soaked our chimneys, put out our water heaters, and turned the clay of the volcanic soil into a slick adhesive our children's shoes got stuck in. Our husbands made a boardwalk of pine trees so we could get from the car to the front door.

Soon the flowers were withering in the hottest, driest days of summer, and we were hot inside our houses and we were hot outside and we were sweaty and the soil clung to our wet arms, to our lips. We tried to read books in the yard or we began a victory garden, planting tomatoes, spinach, green beans, watermelon, and basil to make our rations go further. Though it rained, rapidly, in the midafternoon, we were not accustomed to gardening in a desert climate and we watched as nothing sprouted; we watched as our victory garden did not grow.

There were building crews, bulldozers, cranes, the sounds of trucks, the clouds of dust, the roar of diesel, the chaos that comes with construction. The few dignified, original stone and ponderosa pine buildings — the lodge and a dozen homes — were, within weeks, surrounded by barracks, apartments, Quonset huts, trailers, and prefabricated houses.

At the Housing Office in a piñon-shingled garage next to the water tower on wooden stilts, we argued with Vera, a Women's Army Corps member, who did not want to grant us a bathtub. As politely as we could muster we thanked her for nothing and walked back to what she said was ours — a thin-walled little house. Our loveseats and wingback chairs and record players and books were still all piled in the middle of the living room — we had stalled unpacking in hopes we could persuade the Housing Office we needed one of those stone houses with a bathtub. We plugged in the radio for comfort and heard, for the first time, or the first time in a long time, cowboy music. The jealousy of lost love, the sorrow of being a poor man, men telling women, through jolly beats, to put down their pistols — all of this was interrupted by the news that Mussolini had been arrested. And as we looked around at the only things we had to set up — our dining table, our sickly cactus centerpiece, our dishtowel napkins — we hoped this meant we would not have to stay in New Mexico for very much longer. Five days later Italy did surrender, but several cactus centerpieces would die before we had hope that Germany and Japan might give up.

The sandy soil came through cracks in the windows and doorframes, and gathered on the furniture, the floor, and our Army-issued cots, which were stamped USED. Gusts of sand made outlines of our bodies on the sheets. We stared at the USED stamp at the foot of our beds. Eventually we learned that USED did not mean it was recycled, but stood for the United States Engineering Division. But they were used: our beds still bore the names and ranks of boys who had slept on these mattresses before us, who had carved their names into the frame. What had these beds and these men seen? Where had they traveled?

The small wooden buildings were all painted the same olive color, which matched the dusty pines and in some seasons blended in with the background of the mountains. Green walls, green chimneys, green tin. One of us set a pot of red geraniums in front of the door so our children, our husbands, and ourselves could recognize our home. One of us put a black bowl of pinecones on the porch. Because the streets were not named and the houses were identical, when we met someone at the commissary and invited them over for tea, or for coffee, the only way we could describe our home was in relation to the water tower, the highest thing in town: *West of the water tower, third house on the right. East of the water tower, the last house on the left before the road ends.* It was a landmark that mocked us — a water tower that only sometimes held enough water for us to bathe or flush our toilets.

Our husbands were unshaven and within a few days became bristly; for the first time we could not see their strong jawlines, and their faces moving in close, for a kiss, caused our own to sting.

In that first week we were invited to learn how to run our clothes through the hand-cranked mangle at the community laundry. Before this, we had other people do our laundry, or we had electric wringers, and for many of us our memories of those hand-powered water extractors were of the heavy crank and our mother's warnings not to get our hair caught in it. We were still wearing high heels and they stuck in the mud and we pretended that we learned what we were taught about the mangle but instead gathered our husband's shirts in a wet bundle and carried them home, smiling sourly. We hung the clothes on the line and ironed the cotton shirts on our kitchen table. Because our clothesline was erected in one of the only spots on the mesa that was not in direct sunlight, in the morning we brought our children's cloth diapers and our husband's boxer shorts in as square little ice boards.

It was our first day, our second day, our hundredth day, and bells sounded. Bells sounded in the morning to tell our husbands it was time to go to the Tech Area, bells sounded in the evenings to tell our husbands it was time to get back to the Tech Area after dinner, bells sounded if there was a fire, bells sounded if we were out of water, bells sounded, bells sounded.

IN THE DAY, IN THE NIGHT

Louise played power forward for the University of Nevada's basketball team and helped win the state championship. *She is a great shooter,* her husband bragged. We weren't surprised — she was a tall, strong woman who seemed to find a solution to everything, as if the belief that she could made it so. And though the weekly dust storms got the best of several of us, when it covered her house Louise just hauled her sofa out into the front yard, pounded the couch cushions clean again, and lugged it back inside without complaint. Others of us said, *What's the use?* and only cleaned the sofa when it was our turn to host a party.

Margaret was very pretty, very pregnant, and very helpless. She cried easily — about the dust, the snow, her husband — it did not seem to matter: each day there was something one could be upset about, and she was always upset. She appeared in the evenings puffy-eyed with a scraggly ponytail, dragging herself from the door to the porch post and leaning against it. Her whole body pouted. We

38

guessed a smile had crossed her face on only a few occasions. Since she was our new neighbor we invited her to tea and introduced her to the other girls we were getting to know, but she complained about the same things, again and again, and there was only so much we could do.

Down the street was Katherine, a tall redhead with a thin beak of a nose, who seemed to divine the secret activities in the Tech Area. *Really coming to a boil at South Mesa,* she'd say to us, and sure enough later that afternoon we would hear explosions coming from South Mesa. We never figured out how she knew these things, but we concluded her husband told her. *He must be very important.* Her psychic abilities became even more mysterious when we learned, after the war, that her husband actually had the lowest level of security clearance. *Who was she a private companion to?*

And there was something magnetic about Starla — it was easy to see why Ventura High voted her most likely to be president. She had a way of being friends with everyone while still retaining her own strong opinions. She never told people directly they were wrong, but they were often persuaded by her. In the mornings, just after sunrise, we could see her through our own gauzy, off-white curtains, and through her own, dancing — her daily exercise. She did not move gracefully at all. She was not petite, she sometimes had hamburger stuck between her teeth for whole dinner parties, her arms and legs leaped without any distinguishable rhythm, but she seemed herself somehow, and that was beautiful.

What else were we? Energetic, disheveled, determined, and disagreeable. After teasing our friends' husbands about their politics — either they were too sympathetic of communism, or they were too trusting of capitalism — a flash of anger would cross their faces and they would tell us we were *quite the character*.

When we learned that the Fuller lodge was built by Michigan investors as a resort area but no one wanted to vacation here, we were not surprised. Instead the vacation homes with bathtubs became sleeping quarters for the Los Alamos Boys' School, a place designed to help harden the young boys of elite East Coast and Midwestern families. All those boys sent to the Southwest to be toughened up: boys who would go on to be presidents of Sears, American Motors, Quaker Oats, who would become the owners of the Chicago

White Sox, who would become famous writers of the sixties counterculture. This location of hardening was now ours.

Bathtub Row, Louise deemed those older homes. Those houses were made not with tin and drywall but with stone and hardwood, and also had a claw foot tub, when all we had was a stall shower lined with zinc. Those women — the Director's wife, three women who were also scientists, others who were somehow considered favorites — took baths that most of us could not, those women got a good soak, those women, we told one another, had maid service more frequently than we did. *Those women, those women.* And if our husbands told the Housing Office they needed a bathtub to get new ideas, it was still no use. Our status symbol was who had a bathtub, even though there was rarely enough water to fill it. Because of the water situation, the most impolite thing we could do was flush another woman's toilet. Some of us, the spiteful ones, would use another woman's restroom and exclaim, *Oh my, I can't believe I forgot!* but no one believed them. When we ran out of water, we wore kerchiefs on our heads, or refused to leave the house. And many of us chortled at the wives who would not socialize on account of their dirty hair.

When the water came out of the faucet it often came out brown, sometimes as thick as mud. We were told to take *good citizen showers*, to soap up and then turn on the shower. Many times we got prepared for a *good citizen shower* and the water never appeared. And our bodies were left cold, soapy, and sticky and we never took a *good citizen shower* again.

By late September we got news that though Italy had surrendered to the Allies, German paratroopers had rescued Mussolini and now the Germans occupied Rome, with Mussolini, some said, serving only as the figurehead. Our hopefulness of getting out soon was gone. The dry air cracked our lips and Katherine swore she gained a new wrinkle each month because of it. We applied thick cold cream that made our foreheads shiny and our faces smell like, according to our husbands, *rotting flowers*, and we had to choose between our husbands' noses and our future faces.

In the day we wore gingham, at night we wore our prewar silk stockings, our prewar silk dresses. If we were the same proportions and lived close to one another we swapped clothes to make our own wardrobes appear more extensive. We admired Starla's purple felt swagger brim hat, Louise's ruby feather skimmer, Helen's red-checkered skirt, and Margaret's canary yellow scarf. We had not accounted for the harsh high desert nights and for the first weeks we were cold in our cotton. In the chilly evenings we envied Ingrid's wool cardigan in blush, which we were unable to buy ourselves due to the rationing. And, we could not believe it, but we even envied — on days we carried two armfuls of groceries home after the sun went down — the Army's bulky drab-colored coats.

Many of us hated the women scientists. And the women scientists hated us, or they had better things to worry about. We tried to be their friends. We invited one of them to lunch but she was busy. We despised what she knew and how she laughed at our questions. How she went on hikes with our husbands without us. How she carried herself with the knowledge of things we did not know.

Therefore, a few of us flirted with *her* husband, another scientist, at cocktail parties, after he had two drinks, while she was in the restroom; we flirted until we thought we could have him if we chose, and we winked at her when she returned to the conversation.

Or we tried to keep our enemies closer than our friends. We brought over corn bread. We asked about her daughter, who was homesick, or her son, who was getting in trouble at school. We offered to make soup. We listened.

Or we had little patience for petty competitions for power among women. We were preoccupied instead with the fate of Europe, and with our husbands and other scientists and their wives we talked about the war, Germany, and the suffering the Nazis were bringing into the world.

We did not all agree about the women scientists. Margaret thought Joan Hinton was nice enough, even though most of us said to one another, *Joan Hinton needs to pull down her skirt and stop flirting with Frank.* Frank was Louise's husband. *Oh, Frank.* There was something refined about him, even in the summer with his shirt off, under a car, or playing the guitar. We could tell by how our husbands held their heads when speaking to him that he was respected, even if we did not know exactly what he did. And Frank, unlike our husbands, never seemed fettered, never seemed as if the pressure of this town, or this war, got to him. We, too, lingered on Frank.

FROM FIELDS,
FROM CONCRETE

We were warned by our mothers, our grand-mothers, our uncles, our fathers, our priests, and our rabbis not to marry them before the war was over; they worried we were making a hasty decision; they thought time would change our minds. Our fiancés were men they did not like, or they loved the men we chose but they thought we were too young, or they wanted us to finish college first. And when we did marry them we were told, *Well, Virginia, you'll need a broom and a dustpan.* Perhaps we did not marry our first loves — men who in our memory were reduced to caricature — the athlete, the class clown. We married the scientists instead, men with thick heads and scrawny bodies. Or we had always loved the scholarly ones most of all.

Our husbands came from small towns, from large cities, from fields, from concrete. We met them on boardwalks in Atlantic City, on football fields in Iowa, at cafés in Berlin, at scientific meetings in Moscow. They were disqualified for the draft due to rheumatic fever as a child, diabetes, being overweight, being underweight, asthma, deafness, or poor eyesight. They spoke several languages, they were aggressive at sports, they loped across the street, they shined with knowledge. They thought we were beautiful, they thought we were smart, they thought we had soft breasts, they thought we would make good mothers.

We married them weeks or months after Pearl Harbor — in spring, summer, fall, and winter — when our West Coast hometowns were declared to be in a state of emergency and all citizens had a curfew of ten o'clock. We wore smart white suits, or dresses our mothers made, or dresses we bought in Milan or Paris. We were married in parks, in churches, in synagogues, and in courthouses with our sisters, our mothers, our fathers, and our friends. We were married in the presence of neighbors, distant family members, our mother's bridge partners — people we were obligated to invite though we did not really like them.

In the air was the threat of every man leaving, of every man being a hero, of every eligible bachelor dying — these threats made our fiancés more desirable to us, our love more urgent. We were ready to decide something very large about our futures.

We were featured in the celebrations section of our hometown newspaper with a paragraph about our wedding, what we wore, what we were doing now, and what our parents did. We were Audreys and Susans and we carried bouquets of white orchids surrounded by stephanotis. Our bridesmaids wore French blue chiffon, or gray tulle, and held yellow cascade bouquets of gladiolas and daisies. Or we wore cotton and did not tell the celebrations section that under our dresses were our worn-out saddle shoes. Afterward, we held small receptions at hotels, in church basements, and in our parents' backyards.

Our brothers said we looked like movie stars, like angels, like ourselves, like ourselves but prettier, like our mothers. Or our brothers were late to our weddings because they were taking the officer candidate exam. Or our brothers were not there to see us wed — they were in a bunker in Europe, they were at Army gunnery school. They were Navy bombers, and on our wedding day the newspaper reported: *A Navy patrol plane with ten men aboard has been unreported since it took off on a routine training flight Friday and it is presumed lost in the Gulf,* and we did not hear from our brothers on our wedding day, or the next week, or the next.

47

Our parents cried; our parents' friends told us how much they loved weddings because they got to feel as if they were renewing their own vows, too; we looked around rooms and lawns and churches and we could only see the smiling people, and we felt an abundance of love, though photographs later might show frowns or boredom.

Now we thought we had lost our glow but only from lack of sleep or because of the desert air, and we thought our husbands looked more distinguished these days, or less wild in the eyes, or more so. We felt in control of ourselves, we felt hopeful that we had made the right choice, we felt weary, we felt all these things at the same time, but more so: we felt we could not turn back.

WINTER

Winter arrived and our husbands were issued baggy overalls that came up to their chest and strapped over their shoulders, a heavy down coat, and a snood with a chinstrap. They looked like zoot suits for polar expeditions. Our husbands modeled this outfit, along with their shatterproof glasses and black shoes with thick soles that they said could not conduct electricity. We wondered. Where were the tender bodies of our brilliant husbands?

We tried to forget there was a war going on, and we had our own battles here on the mesa, anyway, but our daily lives were punctuated with news from the outside. British bombers raided Berlin in daylight for the first time and Germany was losing in Stalingrad — these things were hard to picture, so we thought of what we knew of those places before the war, how one summer we walked from one end of Berlin to the other admiring the architecture and history of such an old place; how in the early morning the smell of baked bread wafted through the streets. Berlin, our summer love.

While we slept the snow piled high outside our windows. We woke to see a coyote stretched out on the white lawn and wanted to enjoy this sight with a steaming cup of coffee. But, when we went to pour water into the percolator, only a mud-colored spurt of liquid came out of the faucet, followed by a chugging sound, and then nothing.

We concluded the pipes must have frozen, and we were right: by midmorning we saw the military hauling buckets of water from the Rio Grande, forty miles down the Hill. No coffee for us for a while, nor could we brush our teeth. And though we had escaped the spring and summer sandstorms, the coal that fueled our furnaces was making a thick layer of soot on our cars and our windows. It was as if black muslin lay over the snow.

And when the Jemez was covered with snow we skied on Sawyer Hill with our children while some of our risk-taking husbands, bored by the same pattern of up and down that comes with alpine skiing, gathered groups to go on crosscountry explorations further into the hills. They broke trails, climbed steeper mountains, and were happy when they could come home and announce they had tired out all of the men younger than themselves.

OUR HUSBANDS

Our husbands drew us graphs instead of writing us love notes, graphs that marked their love for us on the y-axis, and our time together on the x-axis, with a line rising exponentially toward an increase in love. Our husbands had salty necks, had holes in their pants. Our husbands were handsome, but their handsomeness was of a different nature now: they had a secret they would not confess. We gave our husbands glances that said we trusted they were making something of themselves.

They were no longer Doctor or Professor, but Mister. Instead of physicists and chemists, our husbands were called fizzlers or stinkers. We knew they worked in a lab, because they called it that at first, but soon the name was changed to the Tech Area. We heard it was dirty inside, that the dress was casual, that the people were talented and strange. They had arithmetic competitions to see who could compute the fastest. They picked the locks of one another's file cabinets to prove they could crack any code. Or instead of appearing competitive about science, our husbands battled fiercely over Ping-Pong. They walked the halls and beat bongos to help them think.

Our husbands said *At any rate*, while we said *Nevertheless*. They doubled back on their thinking — they asserted, then considered, then found something contradictory and refuted what they initially claimed. Their arms gesticulated wildly when they were excited, or had an idea, and we had to be careful that they weren't holding a screwdriver, a drink, or our young children.

Many of them cared a lot about utility and nothing for appearances. If it were their choice our bookshelves, dining room chairs, and coffee tables would all be made of industrial materials like steel. Thankfully for us, these materials were difficult to come by during the war.

At six in the evening they would, usually, drift back from the Tech Area looking wild, talking their own language, *sciencese*, or talking about how to win at poker, or how to hunt wild turkeys. The words we could say became less and less technical and the words we could not say grew larger. We could not say *fission*, a word we overheard often when our husbands were graduate students. Our husbands said *Gadget*, and talked about *issues with the Gadget*, but what *was* the *Gadget*? We did not know. When no one was home we whispered their real names, and our own: *Dr. Fermi, Mrs. Fisher, Enrico, Jane, Jane Marie.*

They squinted. They ate slowly. Their gait was uneven. They stooped. They asked forgiveness rather than permission. Henry with his leather elbow patches. Enrico with his rolled-up khakis. Louis's willowy frame in blue jeans. The Director's black porkpie hat becoming faded and crumpled. Clarence's piano playing, Frank's deep laugh, Paul's shy smile. Our husbands, the only cellist in town. Our husbands, as playful and naïve as our little boys, our husbands deep in thought, our husbands walking into telephone poles, our husbands' ongoing drama of the misplaced reading glasses. From the Alps, from the lowlands. Our husbands returning from canyon hikes with arrowheads and blisters. All of them in silly hats singing at parties with delight, though their voices were bad. Our husbands who rode bikes through the mud and snow and insisted, despite what the General said, that they were not a motley crew.

The General described them as longhairs, for how they did not keep their hair cropped short but instead let it sometimes fall across their foreheads and into their eyes. They said to us, *We aren't oddballs. We aren't a bunch of crazies.* We laughed, or raised our eyebrows, or nodded. Many of us were not the kind to regularly agree with our husbands. Instead when they argued something we found counterexamples and asked questions that would get them caught in their own logical fallacies. They kept us sharp, too, though we complained about their corrections: like how alpenglow was not an *optical illusion* but rather an *optical phenomenon*.

How well our husbands knew science determined their status, which was indicated by how much access they had to secrets. We learned after the war that their security access was marked by the color of their badge. They wore white badges or they wore blue badges; they knew what was going on, or they only knew what they needed to in order to do their job. We knew close to nothing, though we speculated about who knew the most. Many of our husbands were physicists, and some of us guessed by who spent more time thinking than talking who had the high-status position of theoretical physicist. Some men we knew from before Los Alamos and we were happy to see them again. We could remember bits of their previous interests: one had investigated cosmic rays and now spent his days in a shack at the bottom of a canyon, another had conducted experiments related to radioactivity and, like our husbands, went to the Tech Area each morning.

If we invited more people to dinner than we had table space for, our husbands went out an hour before the guests arrived and found a piece of wood, sawed it down, and built an extension leaf. When the scientists, our husbands, arrived to Ingrid's house stomping their boots on the porch and calling to her husband, *Congratulations!* while holding up bottles of liquor, which should have been dificult to find in this time of rationing, we had no idea what they were talking about. Ingrid asked Henry why he was being congratulated, and we asked our husbands why they were congratulating him, but our husbands just shrugged, and then smiled; we scoffed and walked away. We went, next, to one of the female scientists, Irene, a sturdy young girl with short hair and blunt bangs, who was said to have a spectacular IQ; surely another woman would tell us. We asked her, *What's all this about?* And she raised her head, looked down at us — she was quite tall — and said, smiling, *Why, he shot down a Jap battleship!* And earlier that day the Army radio station had reported that the U.S. military destroyed four Japanese carriers and a cruiser, but our husbands had been here all along, and so what that female scientist said was surely impossible. She was pulling our leg, though it felt like more than that.

We thought, *You are making fun of me*, and we concentrated our faces in the other direction so she would not see our wobbly chins, because we were inexplicably starting to tear up, we were becoming too emotional, and she was poking fun at what we did not know and we were losing our wits. *Who cares about her*, we thought. When she turned toward a man with whom she could converse about science, toward our husbands, and our husbands touched her shoulder as they spoke, we told ourselves we hated her.

Before we got married we asked our grandfathers, whose own marriages had lasted forty years or more, *What is the secret to a happy marriage?* And they paused, looked down at their chicken salad, and said, *You have to really like each other. After the attraction, you have to really like the person.*

We crunched our lettuce. Our teeth clinked against the fork. Did we like our fiancés? What does liking someone mean? Before we got married our mothers told us we had to communicate. *Ask him how his day was. Take an interest in his profession.* But we could not do this anymore. Our husbands were gone for twelve hours a day and sometimes did not come home at all. Instead they dragged an Army cot — identical to our own beds — into the Tech Area. And we were not allowed to ask questions.

What did we think our husbands were doing in the lab? We suspected, because the military was involved, that they were building a communication device, a rocket, or a new weapon. We ruled out submarines because we were in the desert — but we closely considered various types of code breaking.

COOKING

The altitude made our breads flat. We requested hot plates, and they arrived, and we carried them with us to parties. Posters of corn that said CORN IS THE FOOD OF THE NATION! lined the Lodge walls and we made so much corn bread, corn cakes, corn casserole, and corn with pepper that we were soon sick of corn.

We named our stoves after an autobiographical memoir told by a horse — one that began with his carefree days as a youth, moved to his difficult life pulling cabs in London, and ended with his happy retirement in the country. All along he recounted tales of cruelty and kindness. We named our stoves Black Beauty and snorted with laughter. Or we called it that because everyone else did, though we did not get the reference, or we refused to call it that. Mostly, we thought our stove was huge and ugly and we only loved it when the electricity went out, because since it was heated with wood and coal, we could still continue cooking dinner even if we had no power. At first, before we became savvy with our stove, we would go without supper. Sometimes there were no lights in the streets, and no flashlights to carry around, and it was dark all through town, but never quiet, and families were reading aloud, and there was candlelight, and we heard the laughter of children being tickled.

Some of us hated the stove situation so much we complained, and we asked for a new stove, an electric one, and if our husbands had high security clearance, something might be done about it. We called the Housing Office and heard the Army man's voice gurgle and we guessed he had been celebrating some small military victory. This seemed to happen every day, but we thought it was really just an excuse to celebrate the enjoyment of liquor. Maybe this time it was something about the Allies landing in Anzio, or some other sign that might indicate we were beating the Germans. Although winning could be worthy of celebration we still needed a new stove.

The Army man said a stove would come that day, and it did not come; he said a stove would come the next and it never came. And therefore it is possible we took matters into our own hands. Late one Sunday night, when the town was still groggy from the weekend, we gathered with Louise, Starla, Ingrid, and Katherine. We made a furniture dolly with two-by-fours, a scrap of carpet, and four wheels borrowed from Louise's sofa. Perhaps we went into the common area and took what we needed, and felt the thrill of doing things we were not supposed to do, and it is possible we experienced this thrill more than once.

FOREIGNERS

Some of us had not always been Americans. Our husbands went from being Hans to Jack, and we went from being Mrs. Mueller to Mrs. Miller. We changed out of slacks and into blue jeans, and already we felt more like Americans. But we were still Europeans, too.

We sat on hay bales in Fuller Lodge and watched short films put out by the War Department that were aired before the featured movies. We wanted to watch *Meet Me in St. Louis* but we had to suffer through films that asked, *Why are we Americans on the march? Pearl Harbor, is that why we are fighting? Or is it because of Britain? France? China?* The list continued for at least ten more countries.

The answer to the question was: *For freedom. They say trouble always comes in threes — look at these faces.* And we saw Mussolini, Tojo, and Hitler at podiums, in front of hundreds of people, speaking. *They gave up their power*, the film said, and *they* meant non-Americans, citizens of other countries. Some of us had extended families that were still in Germany, France, Norway, Poland, Holland, Greece, Belgium, and elsewhere. Or we were born in the U.S. and the film did not seem strange to us.

We were Italians and we clenched our teeth; or we were Germans and we laughed out loud when we heard, *Germans have a natural love of regimentation and harsh discipline*; or we were not surprised. But when the film said, *German defeat was never acknowledged in the last war and they were ready to back anyone who would obtain victory for them*, we wished these silly theatrics would hurry up so we could escape into the stories of *Holiday Inn*, *Slightly Dangerous*, or *My Sister Eileen*. And if we had been brave, if we had wanted to make a scene, to say *This is wrong*, we would get up from our hay bale and walk out. But where would we go and whose mind would it have changed? We would be back in our drafty living room with only our own suffering — missing the film and worrying that our new friends might think us suspect.

GROWING

One spring night we got permission to use a military phone to call the outside world and we stood with our husbands and dialed our parents' number from the military police booth, and we looked up to see what looked like millions of stars, a pointillism we never saw back home and the connection was so scratchy, we weren't even sure it was our mothers on the line or if they could hear us. We yelled, with our husbands, in unison, *We're pregnant!* though of course our husbands were not pregnant, but at that time, before morning sickness, before labor, when our stomachs felt just a little hotter to the touch and only our sense of smell was enhanced, it was as if they, too, were pregnant with us.

Or there was never a time before morning sickness and it did not just occur in the morning.

Sometimes, rather than calling, we wrote to our mothers and they sent back directives: *Wash your feet twice a day. Drink a glass of wine each night. Go to bed hungry. Lots of milk. Lots of activity. Sex, but not in the last trimester. Name him Theodore, after my father. Name her Opal, after your dead aunt. Name him anything but Henry.*

Although we told our mothers immediately, many of us did not tell one another until the fifth month. Maybe we hoped no one would notice until then because we were staying so slender. Or we did not tell because we had lost one before and we did not want to get our hopes up, or anyone else's. We did not want to be offered condolences. We did not want to explain why our bellies were small again, but where was our baby?

Some of us squealed as soon as we missed a period and ran to tell the rest of us. And the second place we might run to was the Housing Office, where we would announce, *I'm pregnant!* or *I'm having another one!* because this might mean we would qualify for a bigger green house. The man at the Housing Office said, *Ma'am, you'll have to wait until we can hear the baby crying before you can fill out one of these forms.*

Our bellies grew. Our husband's spicy scent wafted to us from across a room and Roscoe's litter box stank even when there was nothing in it. We requested our husbands find us milkshakes, iced tea, fried chicken, lemonade, and lentil soup. And some things on this list were impossible to locate, which made our want for them that much stronger, and other things we found rather intolerable — jalapeño peppers, grapefruit — though we loved them before. We swore we would never get pregnant again, and we hated being pregnant in the summer and how our backs ached, and we loved our pregnant bodies, how they made room for another life, how everyone told us we were luminous. We worried about our child having all his fingers and toes, and we sipped more iced tea and hoped he would come out soon. Or we wished it would in fact be a she and that she would get out of us already.

Many of us had due dates just a few days apart and it was comforting to know that Starla, Ruth, Alice, and Louise would all be in the maternity ward, too. What a calming thought to walk out of the house with nothing to do except this: give birth. The idea of two weeks in the hospital — a break from cooking, cleaning, and hosting — meant having someone wait on us: nurses bringing us dinner, bathing our babies, changing our sheets, and monitoring our health. It would be a vacation! Louise said, *It's enough of an incentive to keep me pregnant for a lifetime.*

We held and received baby showers almost weekly, in rooms of tissue paper flowers and pink, yellow, or blue streamers. Some of us thought it was bad luck to buy anything before the baby was born, but others of us thought it was morbid not to and we extended our morning coffee by leafing through catalogs of strollers and bassinets. Though our homes were temporary, we wanted to paint, choose a crib, and consider wallpaper. Polka dots, stripes, flowers. We were told red was the first color a baby could see, and we thought we could use that as an accent color, but when we saw the red samples at a hardware store in Santa Fe we thought, *blood, our brothers, the war*, and changed our minds.

Our children came fast and two weeks early, came in the backseat before our husbands could get out of the driveway, on the bathroom linoleum we had installed ourselves. We went into labor in the kitchen, and our neighbor came to help us, and someone else ran to get our husbands from the Tech Area. And when our husbands came home they heard the first earthly wails of their new daughters, their new sons, their twins, and we saw terror and awe in their eyes.

Or we gave birth in Army sedans on our way up the Hill, or at the hospital, right on time. A few of us pretended that we felt no pain as the contractions grew more painful, and we smiled serenely when our friends checked in on us. Or when our husbands came to see us on their lunch break we howled and they kissed our foreheads and apologized and said they were sorry but they had to get back to the Tech Area. And if this was our first birth, the pain we knew before contractions was actually not pain at all and most pain after childbirth was nothing. We learned labor was not generally a place for modesty, and if we were in the ward together we helped one another with compresses and conversation as best we could.

Sometimes our husbands were not allowed in our rooms even if we begged for them, and if they were allowed they came in running, looking more terrified than we felt, and it was us who had to comfort them, saying, between contractions, *I'm fine. Really.*

Or our due date came and went. We walked to the hospital, lay down, were gassed and cut open. We wanted to squat but were instructed to lie flat on our backs so the doctor could reach the baby more easily. We longed for our midwives trained in Tuskegee, who relaxed us by massaging our legs, who told us what to expect. We did not want drugs, but we were put under, and we have no memory of labor, except when we heard a cry, and being startled awake by the smell of coffee, and someone saying: *It's a beautiful girl!* or, *It's a handsome boy!* behind the first yowls of our newborns.

Or the room was silent and someone said, *I'm sorry.*

We named them James, Patricia, Mary, Robert. We named them Linda, William, Richard, Shirley. Betty, Diane, Harold, Douglas. Brenda, Frances, Carolyn, Henry. When we began there were twenty of us, then fifty, then the number of us grew too large to count, and in the first year alone we gave birth to eighty healthy children.

The General complained to the Director, *Too many babies! They are taking advantage of us! You've got to do something about this.* The Director replied, casually, *I'm not going to interfere in the lives of adults.*

HELP

We longed for our mothers, who would console us, who would watch our children so we could take a shower, so we could go out with our husbands on a date, so we could take a walk without a hundred necessities that had to be met. We wanted help. Someone to wash the windows, the dishes, the bathroom. Someone else to use the mangle, someone else to iron our husbands' shirts.

Eventually help came. They had glossy hair cropped at their chins. They had long dark hair pulled back or let loose. Some of us called them girls, the girls, except for Katherine, who called the girls *helps* and announced she should have as many helps as she was willing to pay. According to Ronnie, who was keen to the cost of everything, they earned three dollars per day.

They were Tewa women from the nearby San Ildefonso and Santa Clara pueblos who arrived by bus in the morning and disappeared by bus at night. Or they were Spanish women whose family homestead was nearby, or they were sixteen-year-old girls from St. Catherine's Indian School coming up from Santa Fe.

We now had help, but there were saints' days and feast days and the days leading up to them when the girls stayed at home to prepare. Since we did not celebrate these days, we found it hard to keep track of when they occurred, and it was not easy to find out in advance how many days they would be gone. We sometimes marched into the Maid Services Office and demanded to know why no girls arrived, only to be told it was a holiday.

They were our nannies, our maids, and our extended family members. They did not look like us and we hated them. They seemed content and beautiful and we loved them. They were just people like anyone else and we felt thankful to have them around. They were our Florencitas and Rosalies — who gave us black pottery for Christmas, who brought us thin tortillas made from blue corn and pottery candlesticks in the shape of high pueblo boots, who left us notes apologizing that they could not wash the bedsheets because our husbands were in them.

They gave us loaves of round bread baked in their beehive ovens. They were heedless of our instructions to vacuum the Oriental rugs and instead dragged them out on the back porch and shook them above the heads of the children playing below. One of the girls asked Katherine, whom she thought of as not only her boss but her friend, to bake one of her famed stuffed chickens for a celebration. Katherine did so, but said to the rest of us: *Just who is working for whom?*

We thought them generous and good with our children. We learned how to swaddle our babies as they did. We tutored their sons in English after school and they taught us how to make more northern New Mexico dishes — tortillas, posole, and corn cooked the Indian way. They learned to make our peanut butter sandwiches, but we never learned the delicious secret of their *kapo-wano* fried bread.

As we ate breakfast we saw the group of women walking past the water tower and to our houses, dressed in colorful mantas tied with woven belts, high white deerskin boots or plain walking shoes, with shawls over their heads and shoulders, and *so much turquoise,* we told one another. *Enough to stock a trading post.* When we noticed that the bus delivered them an hour before the shift started, some of us invited them in for coffee on cold days. And as we made oatmeal we heard them speaking quickly and giggling in the living room, but we never found out what was so funny. Though most knew three languages — English, Spanish, and their native Tewa — many talked little to us.

Others of us made closer friendships. On her way to the dorms where she worked, Ana stopped to talk about mesa affairs. Later on, when she started taking her lunches at our house, we sat and gossiped. A few of us learned about some young Indians' thinking: how they wanted to remain in the pueblo but desired a better life for their children than they had. How the old people wanted to keep things as they were. Ana was saving money for a new house with an inside bathroom, good heating, and an icebox like the Army provided for us. Julieta, on the other hand, resisted such improvements, considering them unnecessary.

One girl told us that each time the General came to the pueblo to recruit them for work he wore khaki shorts. The tribal members gave him a Tewa nickname — a word we can't recall — and he seemed very proud to have his own special name. *What did the name mean?* we asked our housekeeper. She smiled and said, *The man who wears baby pants.*

When we were invited to feast days it seemed strange to us to watch the corn dancers bring the Catholic saint from the church and place it in a shrine set up for the day, then perform the ancient dances that seemed to have no relation to Christianity. When the dancers stopped to rest, they had a choice of going into the kiva or kneeling in the shrine to pray before the saint. At sunset the dancers, still in corn dance costume, carried the saint back to the church. We asked, *How can you be good Catholics and also believe in your traditional gods?* Ana saw nothing strange or contradictory — this, she said, was the way it had always been. But by asking Anita, an Indian who sometimes spoke in Fuller Lodge about Indian customs, we learned of the pueblo's two rebellions against Spanish rule and their centuries of cohabitation.

We asked Apolonia what her husband did for work. *He does the hunting.* Now they were buying food from the commissary, so we asked again, *What does your husband do now?* She replied, *I give him money. He goes to the store and buys the food.* It could have been more complicated than these chosen words, there may have been things she could not or would not articulate about her relationship with her husband, but we did not press her.

She asked us what we were doing here in the desert. We said, *The war.* She nodded and we interpreted this as disapproval, so we said, *Do you know why we are fighting?* She said *No,* or she said *Yes,* but either way we could tell it did not matter. We told her a story — of surprise attacks, victims, greed. *Well, what do you think of the war now?* we asked, feeling we'd done a particularly good job of conveying the atrocities. She gave us a look. Her opinion had not changed.

And why should it have? Were we blind to the struggles of others? First the Spaniards, then the Anglos, then the Mexicans — so many people trying to change them, kill them, and claim the land.

Some of us never talked to our housekeepers, or when we did we talked really slowly and really loudly. We climbed sacred mountains, stood on ceremonial structures, took arrowheads from ancient dwellings for souvenirs, and admired the views. Others of us grew protective of the petroglyphs. When Starla learned that her Henry's favorite mushroom hunting grounds — where he gathered paper bags full of button fungi — was just below a plumed serpent carved in the rock, which could be seen well when the shadows fell, she gave him quite a scolding. Henry had never noticed it, never looked to see the numerous other carvings. Frank added that the living Indians intrigued him far more than the dead ones.

How much did we want them to stay exactly as we had imagined they had always been? Some of us said, over the ladies' lunch, that others of us were *going native*. They were living in a past our ancestors had given up. We were women wanting the girls, who now wore attire similar to our own, to paint the most authentic images, to make the most traditional bowls. What could they do but accommodate us, their patrons.

Though we benefited from their inexpensive domestic help, we still complained that the help was not enough. And it was not fair that some of the girls picked favorites, how they disliked being moved around on the chart each day, and some of us said they just went wherever they pleased anyway. We wanted more help or different help and we were told if we wanted more assistance we would need to have another baby. We complained to our husbands, but they instead tried to find solutions, or joke, rather than listen. They said, *In the future there will be trained chimpanzees mopping our floors, and what the Maid Services Office really should do instead is set up an Agency of Primate Distribution.*

Our husbands parodied our maids in after-dinner skits; our husbands wore scarves on their heads and peasant skirts, turquoise bracelets clinking as they dusted the same table over and over again, as they pretended to be Sofia and took nips of our liquor. We laughed, we cackled, we thought it all in good fun.

A GOOD WIFE

Before we arrived at Los Alamos as wives and mothers we had been teachers in Seattle, housewives in New Jersey, water-colorists in Nebraska, writers in Des Moines, chemists at Harvard, and one of us had been a dancer in the Chicago ballet. Ingrid, Marie, Pauline, and Marjorie all had B.S.s in mathematics with minors in home economics. We were halfway through school when our husbands asked us to marry them, and it didn't seem there was a point in continuing: few married women had careers, and our family did not need the extra income. Or we had once wanted to pursue doctoral degrees but were told by our male mentors during our senior year of college, *There is no place in higher mathematics for women, no matter how brilliant.* Some of us were told, *The universities won't want you, and you'll be over-qualified to teach high school.* Many of us did not pursue a doctoral degree but married a man who got one instead. But a couple of us were encouraged to keep going, or kept going despite what our mentors told us, and we, too, became doctors.

And now here there were jobs for us. The Director came to our house and asked us to *Please think about working while you're here, it would be a good career opportunity*. And if that failed to get a yes, if we lowered our heads and said, *Sorry, no, thanks*, he replied, *Consider the war.*

Our husbands were great physicists and we were considered great secretaries. Or we were hired because the military questioned our moral backbone and wanted to keep us out of mischief. And as secretaries we prepared and filed personnel cards, or stamped *SECRET* in red on medical records. We knew first who was moving to another division in the lab and who had an inexplicable rash. Our husbands appeared to know nothing so we were always telling them the news, despite the fact that they were the ones doing important things in the Tech Area.

We were quite happy to peek inside the secret lab, to make a little bit of money, and to share in the war effort. And when we got inside the infamous Tech Area to begin our job as secretary, or calculator, it was, like most things one builds up in one's imagination, disappointing. The mystery and glamor we'd fabricated was instead a dirty, cluttered, overcrowded mess. But the interior was quickly overlooked by the exciting tempo, casual attire, and jovial atmosphere. Someone was always pulling a practical joke. One bored scientist asked the operator to page Werner Heisenberg, which she did for three days straight — Heisenberg never materialized — until someone told her she'd have to page Berlin instead, as Herr Heisenberg was a famous German physicist working for the other side.

Our first bosses felt that they needed to explain a few things to us and said, *Some of the men are exposed to radiation due to tube alloy,* and we asked, *What's tube alloy?* They blushed and told us to ask our husbands. We knew our husbands: if we were to ask them, they would just give us a mischievous grin. So we did not learn what tube alloy was until much later.

We were secretaries for three hours, six days a week, or we were teachers for eight hours, five days a week. Without any special degree or education, many of us were given the lowest form of security clearance and learned very little of interest. As lab technicians we were paid seventy percent of what a man would make in our position, and the cost of maid services would not be added on to our own salary. When we did the math, we discovered that our family would make only ten percent more a year if we worked than if we did not work. Several of us decided it was too much of a hassle, and we said, *No, thank you,* to the job offers. Lucille and Patricia said, *No.* Katherine, speaking for a large group of us, said, *We have babies to take care of.* Some of us tried it for a week and quit, ultimately choosing to stay home. And we got others to follow us.

If we were British we were not given clearance to work in the Tech Area, and we were told we could not teach school because our upbringing was *very different than the American way,* and we did not want to organize a library for residents who were tired of having to go to the one in Santa Fe to get their books. We were busy enough with our jobs as mothers, housekeepers, wives, and social organizers.

One Brit, Genevieve, could not be busy enough. She left her house every morning to visit the other wives on the mesa, to share advice or receive it; or she left town on the bus with an empty bag and returned in the evening with a full one, bringing back a low-point pot roast bought in Santa Fe and announcing a dinner party. She loved a bachelor with a cold, because it meant she could feed and mother him.

If we declined working we were accused of disloyalty to our country. Our husbands said we were being obstinate. Or our husbands said we did not have to do anything we didn't want to. We worried that if we said yes our home would suffer, our husbands would feel neglected, and our children would become delinquents.

Or we had taught college-level history classes when we were graduate students at Yale, and now we were teaching the children of Nobel laureates, but some of our best students were the children of mechanics. It was not fun to wrangle teenagers who were much more interested in passing notes than history.

Or we would have worked — we'd been a telephone operator once — but our husbands did not think it was a good idea, they thought wives should stay home, and we could see their point to some degree, and though we wanted to get out of the house, though our children were away at school most of the day, though we were stirring, stirring, all day, alone, though it would have been better for us, we did not work.

We had degrees in chemistry and when we said, *Okay*, thinking we would get a chance to do real research in the Lab, we were asked to take a typing test. And that's when we said, *No*. We said, *No*, and we were punished with less help. We were tired of being told by men what to do and we said, *No*. Or we had two toddlers and were not interested in a career in science anymore.

Those of us who worked did so because we were curious or bored, or we did not know how to decline the offer and not feel guilty. And if we did work we were told on our first day not to ask any questions and we didn't — much.

We were mail carriers and we took long trips down winding cliffs to gather the mail in Santa Fe, escorted by an armed guard. We had mailbags locked to our wrists, and only one person — another woman — had the key. We were scolded by the other women if we did not deliver all the mail immediately. We monitored each piece of outgoing mail and sometimes corrected the grammar, or let the writer know that though she said a check was enclosed, she had forgotten to include it.

We worked in rooms full of only women and we were called calculators. We sat six to a table at calculating machines and processed ten- to fourteen-digit numbers. We clanked and banged continuously. We solved differential equations without access to the physics behind them. We made plots of French curves. Eventually, IBM equipment replaced us. We thought our biggest accomplishment was not our calculations, but the survival of our families in this wild military camp.

As part of a volunteer community protection team, we issued passes to new residents and listened for spies, though we had no idea what we were listening for. We were given a list of watchwords, words we had been hearing around town already. *Uranium. Fission. The Gadget.* We were told to look for nervousness, to listen for inflection, and we thought we would be brilliant at this kind of work: we had a lifetime of experience in paying attention. But we never caught a spy.

Some of us did things no one will ever know about because we did not discuss our jobs with anyone. There was a fracture: the tired wives who worked in the Lab and had security clearance and the tired wives who did not work in the Lab. We all worked, of course, cleaning, cooking, bathing, loving, but some of us fabricated lenses using molds that reminded us of cookie cutters. Louise went into labor while at work but monitored her contractions with a stopwatch and still finished her experiment before leaving the Tech Area.

We were scientific librarians, personal secretaries, switchboard operators. The Director gave us fatherly advice about the pressures of wartime marriages. We sang *Happy Birthday* to senior scientists over the PA system.

And after our shift Clara came by and asked us what we did all day and we shrugged, noting how we hated that shrug from our husbands, how we were doing the thing that annoyed us the most, but Susie was polite and knew we could not say and therefore did not ask us. At night we were exhausted and told our husbands, *What I need is a good wife*.

WHEN THE GROUND TREMBLED

Though we no longer kept our fingernails clean, many of us still measured our waist each morning. We wanted to accentuate broad, wide shoulders, which we rarely had. We wore trousers and wedges and boots because we were often on the side of the road with blown-out tires. We still had our fur coats, which lost tufts if we were not careful, but most of us were careful because we knew replacements were impossible. Because buttons were popping off our children's clothes and getting lost in the mud, we switched to zippers.

We forgave one another in public, quickly, even if we did not truly feel the forgiveness in our hearts. And even if we did not fully forgive, we still brought over soup and muffins when their children were sick, because we saw how Geraldine was cut off from afternoon cocktails at Katherine's for, as Katherine said, *flirting with her Charlie*; we saw how Grace was snubbed for not sending a written thank-you note after a dinner party Edna hosted. We knew these isolations would keep us out of knowing things. We did not want to be like Florence, pretending we had to weed in the yard all afternoon because no one invited us over.

We needed more information, or we were concerned our children would not have any other children their age to play with, or we were bored but not lonely, or we were desperately lonely.

We went to Lisa, one of our old friends from Chicago who happened to be sent here, too, and told her our grudges, one at a time. Katherine couldn't see why kindergarten would not take her child even though he was not potty-trained. Rose complained that Starla was taking a lead role in the social activities while *she* was surely the better qualified.

Many of us preferred the wives who seemed to have natural curiosity, who asked, *How do you think that is constructed?* and instead of calling for their husbands to fix the stove, pulled it out from the wall and first attempted to discover how it operated on their own.

At night, as our husbands snored, we read books on loan to us from friends, sent to us

86

by our parents, checked out from the library, mailed to us as part of our Book-of-the-Month Club subscription. We read stories of women who followed their husbands on unknown adventures, like Osa Johnson's *I Married Adventure*, about a Kansas teenager who married a photographer. Together they traveled to Borneo, Kenya, and the Congo, then, in their fifties, near retiring, pondering whether they should have had children, their commercial flight to California crashed. Her husband died, but Osa lived another twenty years. Had we married *mis*adventure? Because we were no longer state citizens, we could not legally vote, get divorced, or obtain a fishing license in the state of New Mexico.

The Stranger, The Little Prince, For Whom the Bell Tolls, Madame Bovary, Native Son, The Grapes of Wrath. Deep within ourselves, we were waiting for something to happen. Our greatest, grandest, most prolonged story: waiting. At times, we became tired from the reading, we wished the next day was already over. But eventually the muscles in our necks relaxed and we slept.

Mornings we woke and hoped something would arrive for us, but rarely did anything arrive. Because we felt powerless, we went to war over milk shortages, water shortages, maid services, and unfair housing assignments. We said, *Someone with one child should not have more help than someone with two.* We said, *A family that needs only two bedrooms should not get a home with three.* The commissary should carry bottled artichoke hearts, the movie schedule should be changed, the neighbor's dog snapped at our child and should be put down, we need a shoe repair service, we need faster mail service, the public laundry is overcrowded, the rifle range is too close.

We threatened to strike unless more maids became available. We tried to master cooking on a temperamental stove but we had no eggs and we howled until the veterinarian brought us some. We commissioned our boys to build us a golf course and when we needed to make a fence around it we stole wire from the Army supply office. We created an orchestra, a square dance club, a jazz band, and a tennis court. We got things by calling a meeting. We got things by being devious.

When the ground trembled and the air smelled like fireworks we knew our husbands, or the military, were trying out explosives. The scent got on our clothes and we could smell sulfur on our hair for days. We tried to control our responses to the sounds in the distance, how they brought the war in close to us and made us worry and we said we would no longer let them do that, even when they rattled our walls, we must not get too upset. We tried to control our impulse to shudder and then one day we noticed we no longer asked *What was that?* and neither did our children.

TALK

We drew closer and lowered our voices.

We began by saying what seemed like nice things. *Shirley looked pretty in her white gloves today at the commissary.* But that compliment suggested other things, that Shirley was stuck-up, that Shirley thought she was too good to be seen with dirty fingernails like the rest of us.

To make oneself the hero through a pregnant pause. We leaned in close to hear more, our eyes alight. *And then what happened, and then what happened.*

We moved from saying nice things to suggesting the not so nice: *Did you see the priest whispering in Dorothy's ear last night? Don't you think he was standing awfully close?*

And later, as we got to know one another better, as we became bored, as we continued to dislike ourselves, or as we became frustrated with being stuck in this town for so long, or we could no longer hold in the secrets that we did know, we said the obviously not nice.

We talked about Jack's wandering eye and William's wrinkled, high-waisted slacks. One of us said, *The General would do anything for a chocolate turtle — I heard he keeps a stockpile of them locked in his safe.* One of us said, *I smelled liquor on Mrs. Oppenheimer's breath at breakfast on Tuesday.*

We told these stories at each other's kitchen tables, the same Army-issued square tables and the same stiff chairs we had ourselves. We felt savvy and funny — leaning in to Esther, to Patti — entertaining them with what we had heard, or suspected. It was like the beginning of a love story, these intimacies, and we had missed them since we'd moved. We shifted from talking about people in power — the Director, the General — to talking about husbands, and finally, to talking about one another. We speculated on who was depressed, who was disappointed, who was deranged, who was playing the game of Musical Beds. *Mary has not washed her hair in a week. Tom has another family in San Antonio. Lisa disappeared with Jack at the Director's party last night.*

We talked about who got their hair color from a bottle — insisting we would never — and who let the delivery boy put his hand on her knee. They kept us awake at night, these rumors, and they brought some of us closer together, and they built trust, or destroyed it, and they passed the time. Because of the lack of insulation in the duplexes and apartments, at least one of us could hear which man cussed at his wife or which man slapped his children after dinner. We knew which woman burst into tears when a military patrolman mentioned his concern about the increase in syphilis cases. We knew which woman disappeared when she was accused of telling secrets. We got our information from the GIs, from our maids, from our cooks, and later, from our own children, but we rarely got anything from the female scientists, or from our husbands, who were the ones who actually knew all the *real* secrets. Everything else we knew in about an hour.

We were a group of people connecting both honestly and dishonestly, appearing composed at dusk and bedraggled at daybreak, committed, whether we wanted it or not, to shared conditions of need, agitation, and sometimes joy, which is to say: we were a community.

1944

INTIMACIES

It was the time of year when the burrowed passions grow arms and legs — they have woken up, they have started to stir. Violence, thirst, and restraint had wintered away. It was the time when windows are left ajar and a person desires to exit rooms through those windows, and does. Around us, at night, above us, in the apartments, wafting through our windows: the beds creaking.

It was Sunday; spring light slanted onto cheeks, with time there had grown a certain looseness to our talk. Starla wanted to discuss the nature of love and said as much by asking, as she looked up from her gimlet, to Dorothy, and then Stan, the newcomers, *How did you two meet?* It was a seemingly innocuous question. Stan ran his hand across Dorothy's arm. They smiled as couples do. Perhaps this was what Starla wanted: to hear a story that would break her heart.

The heavy snow of winter gave way to abundant wild-flowers. Purple pasques blanketed the melting slopes. Though we grew from five to at least fifteen hundred people in one year's time, and we soon felt we knew everybody, of course it was not so. The town felt like ours and we called it Shangri-La, or Sha-La for short, a name we meant, at different moments, both in earnest and in jest.

We lived in Los Alamos but we simultaneously lived elsewhere. The past in Chicago, the future in Cologne. Our differences were heightened by proximity. *The McDougalls have a new Cadillac!* one of us exclaimed, first to our husband, who did not even look up from his newspaper. Our rents were ten percent of our family salary no matter what we lived in, so some of our rents were more expensive even though we all had the same tiny houses, and some of us paid more money for smaller homes just because we did not have two children.

The town grew quickly — we'd go out for a walk, pick lilies for a flower arrangement, and come back to find that our street was expanded another block, four new trailers were installed, and families were already inside, at the dinner table, eating jellied chicken.

Some of us tried visiting with everyone but did not realize we were being talked to as a boss, as a white person, as a wealthy person, as a woman, as a mother, as a European, as an American, which is to say we were not getting the whole story. People protected their intimacies from us, as we did, too.

We felt close enough to our maids to make confessions, to tell them things we would not tell one another. We believed our maids felt equally as close to us — we did not think we had disrupted their lives or uprooted them from their homes. We thought the Indians, especially, loved their daily trips to this other world. The extra money was more than they had ever had, and with it they could afford new additions to houses, new furniture, even a few inside bathrooms. Some of our husbands wired the pueblo for electricity, and soon refrigerators and appliances appeared. When we were invited to the pueblo, many of us were still rather shocked to find Grand Rapids furniture, brass bedsteads, soda pop, and ordinary dishes in the Indian houses. Our houses had more Indian rugs, pottery, and paintings than their own homes had. Some of us set our tables with Maria's famous black plates and candle-sticks, but we noticed that Maria herself set her own table with store-bought tablecloths and dishes.

Some of them had traveled even farther than us, going to London, Paris, Rome, Berlin, and Coney Island while their husbands danced the Eagle Dance on stages for white people. The girls told us that Europeans generally clapped louder than Americans. They told us their husbands did not dance the Eagle Dance the way they did in the pueblo — their faces were not painted, for instance, and they used any kind of feathers they found along the way.

The valley below Los Alamos was an area inhabited by Spanish Americans for hundreds of years and by Indians for tens of thousands of years. Some of our maids' husbands were ranchers or herders until their grasses withered. They came from the valley with trailers that had chimneys, called sheep camps. Some of their husbands were men with hair parted down the middle and two long fishtail braids tied with yarn, or hair kept short in the style given to them in Indian boarding schools, or hair they cut themselves, more stylish than our husbands'. Their husbands ladled soup in our cafeterias. Their husbands changed our lightbulbs, twisted metal wires in the Tech Area, were bitten by our dogs when they came for the trash. Later, when we saw these same men at their ceremonial dances, in fancy costumes and beating drums, they were completely different people to us.

And when the Army issued orders in the *Daily Bulletin* that anyone who did not live on the site could not purchase items at the commissary, we saw that the only people this really excluded were the girls. Even if the Army did have trouble keeping up with our growing population, we protested, these women still needed a way to purchase food for their own families. There were no stores in the pueblos, and since the women worked all day for us, they could not go to Española or Santa Fe to buy things. The Army reversed the ban and we were glad, although the maids often cut short their afternoons to go shopping before the buses left, which did not please many.

We were white and said, *I love how here no one is aware of any color differences, everyone is treated the same.* Some women were not white, or not white in the same way, and they disagreed completely, but in public nodded in agreement. And when our maids moved to the Hill and went to our school to register their children, some of us put their light-skinned children with our light-skinned children and put their dark-skinned children in different classes some of us called the Mexican classes.

Their teenagers were our guards. Their young boys were our hospital orderlies and our messengers. When their sons or husbands were drafted we thought of our own young boys, or our own husbands, or we thought of theirs — our messengers, our hospital orderlies — and how they could be drafted though they could not vote in state or national elections. We helped to find workarounds — drafting them to Los Alamos instead — and if we couldn't help, we cried together over the kitchen sink. But there were still some of us that did not think there was anything wrong with such laws.

MILITARY

We understood why the military hated us.
While their friends were off seeing action in
the Pacific or Europe, their job here was to
protect our husbands, who did not want to be
protected, and to safeguard a secret they did
not know quite how to watch over, since they
did not know what it was.

The military officially ran the town in one
way, and our husbands in practice ran the
town in some ways, and we ran the town
clandestinely in others. The flare of trumpets
awoke us at sunrise on weekends, and we
were annoyed, because the weekends were
our only chance at sleeping in. The troops
eternally paraded and marched; we heard the
steady beat of their boots, their *Hut!* their
Attention! as they turned. They were men just
a bit younger than our own husbands,
sometimes just ten years older than our sons,
with soft baby faces and young eyes that
looked out under stiff hats.

Unlike our husbands, the military men could
not bring their wives to Los Alamos. They

said to us, *What makes you so special?* We said the Army ruled the Hill as if it were a fascist country — controlling when we could leave, where we could live, how much help we got, and what we ate. They were our number one complaint — how they made us fill out dozens of forms, in duplicate, just to get a new lightbulb.

We could not often be mad at them directly because we needed them for furniture, appliances, and food. We blamed them for what went wrong because we needed someone to blame, because we could not blame our husbands. But when the washing machines broke down and the General accused us of abusing them we had something to say: *Have you ever done your family's laundry, General? No? Thought not. We are not the ones to be accused of abuse.*

We argued, unreasonably, that the Army men had more money for new cars, because they always seemed to have them. Or maybe because they could not bring their wives they did not have them around to insist on home decorations — new linoleum, new curtains — and so did in fact have more to spare. They did not have to answer to a wife regarding their spending habits and so they did just what they wanted and bought a new car.

And though our medical services were free, our doctors were Army doctors, and we had no choice about which doctor we preferred to see, but they weren't so bad, and we joked privately over how these Army doctors had signed up to heal soldiers in battle and instead got us — a bunch of high-strung, healthy women complaining of headaches and morning sickness.

The General never missed an opportunity to say he, too, was a scientist, because he had obtained an undergraduate degree in engineering at West Point and had been the project manager for the construction of the Pentagon. He made it clear he did not want us here. He thought we would cause trouble, he thought we would be a distraction. And he wanted our husbands in uniform, beneath him, not wearing jeans, but they had refused to come on those grounds, and the General had to relent and instead our husbands stayed civilians, and we came along.

If it was evening when the military police stopped us, we had trouble holding our skirts down in the wind. We fumbled in our purses.

They leaned in close to hear us say the most beautiful-sounding word in the English language: their own name.

We had a fondness for the engineering division, who were the military, too, but only because they were forced to be. They were men with undergraduate degrees in engineering, and surely they annoyed MPs and sergeants with their disheveled look — their sloped shoulders from stooping over a table all day, their thick glasses, their gangly bodies with paunchy stomachs. And when they marched on weekends with the rest of the military, they were placed in the back as the caboose, and each of their steps was miraculously out of sync with the others.

For some of us, the proximity to a large number of single men revived our girlishness, and we curled our hair, or ironed it, applied lipstick, and smiled at ourselves in the mirror: to have a husband and a fantasy, to be admired at the age of twenty-six, twenty-nine, thirty-three, this felt like a good thing.

WOMEN'S ARMY CORPS

On Monday mornings the trashcans outside the WACs' dorms were full of Coors beer cans. There were three hundred WACs and they had showers and two bathtubs to share among themselves, which they told us about on several occasions. Their hair could not touch their collar; they wore beige skirts and oxfords.

At night we could hear them gathered around campfires singing songs we did not know the names of but once they were in our heads we could not get them out:

> They get us up at five A.M.
> To scrub the barracks clean.
> Then what do we do when we get through?
> We scrub the damn latrine!

and when we were certain we could not take any more singing about military life we heard them marching and chanting:

> Duty is calling you and me.
> We have a date with Destiny.

Ready, the WACs are ready.
Their pulses steady, the world set free.

Their voices carried as they marched from the campfire to their dorm door and into their rooms.

There was not a bed check on Saturdays and on their days off they went to Santa Fe, perhaps watching the sunset on the roof of the La Fonda hotel, as we wished we could. One WAC, Pat, was rumored to, on her breaks, sleep in the stable next to the horses.

Some were Texans who said *little bitty* and *right nice* and had names like Bobbie-Joe and Jimmie. Or they were former schoolteachers named Esther or Marian, from Indiana or Illinois, who said joining the Women's Army Corps was the right thing to do. They organized the motor pool, shot dice, played the pump organ at church services, and called our husbands over the townwide intercom by their last names — *Mitchell, Farmer, Perlman* — but more frequently, about ten times a day, they called out *Gutierraz* and *Marsh* — the two maintenance men. They operated the telephones, censored our mail, and ran the PX, the diner where our husbands got their afternoon coffee and listened to the jukebox. They said they were proposed to once a month because there were ten military men on the Hill to every one of them.

THAW

In April the cottonwoods in the valley began showing their green buds and the commissary carried huge hams for Easter. We reserved Fuller Lodge for Passover seder and prepared hundreds of matzo balls that the chef boiled in water instead of chicken stock. People said they tasted *Excellent!* but they did not. The chaplain, who was not asked to speak, gave a long talk about marauding tigers in India. We said it was a SNAFU, his speech and the matzo balls, an acronym we learned from the military: *Situation normal, all fouled up*.

If we were the proper type, we finally broke down and bought a pair of blue jeans, a jean shirt, and boots so we could ride the horses. The mountains still smelled to us like lavender and lemon verbena, and we hiked the Valle Grande, a mountain meadow the size of Manhattan that in spring became a purple field of wild irises. When we stopped walking we could hear the snakes rattling in the sagebrush.

We took the horses down Frijoles Creek for fourteen miles before arriving at the meandering Rio Grande. We watched the migration of sandhill cranes, admired the fading blue color of the piñon jay, avoided the swimming garter snakes, and were grateful to see a group of mule deer fawns before they lost their spots. Tarantulas with orange tufts on their back ends walked along our hiking trails on warm spring days, but we were not scared. And though we feared mountain lions, black bears, and bobcats, their sightings were mythical.

We carried oats for the horses and sausage and whiskey for us. We got drunk quickly from being so high up in the mountains and sometimes, we are sure, we acted strange or delightful. We called one another's names and reached out our hands for the flask. We rode at night, even when it was raining, even when we were on a mountain ridge in the middle of a thunderstorm, in lightning. One night, after a long afternoon trip turned into an evening outing, with a full moon illuminating our trail, Alice said, *Which way should we go?* and we looked at her but did not reply. She continued, *This way it's only seven miles home*, and pointed to the left. *And this way is longer but much more beautiful*, she said, and pointed to the right. We took the path to the right. And when we came home late, it was our husbands this time who walked out onto the porch as they heard our boot steps, folded their arms over their chests, and scowled. We laughed and said, *Oh, Richard!*

THE DIRECTOR

The Director getting down on one knee to talk to us, because we were sitting. The Director hosting dinner parties — making arugula and mint salad with an impossible-to-find pecorino cheese, creating prosciutto-and-gruyère-stuffed ravioli, presenting us with English plum pudding — dishes he claimed to have learned to make from *the best chef in Italy, the grandest dame in Britain*, or *the finest lady from Arkansas*, as he winked at us.

He was our center of attention, quietly. He did not shout but something about him demanded we listen. Six feet tall and stooped, lanky and shifty in any seat. Oppy, Oppie, Opje — we were awed by his erudition, we were charmed by his elegance, we were chilled by the sarcasm he directed at those he thought of as shoddy or slow thinkers. Our husbands said, *The man is unbelievable! He gives you the answer before you can even formulate the question.*

And because he spoke eight languages he could recite poems to us in our mother tongue. He told us that *À la Recherche du Temps Perdu* — *In Search of Lost Time* — changed the course of his life. He spoke passionately about why he got involved in the war: *I began to understand how deeply political and economic events could affect men's lives. I began to feel the need to participate more fully in the life of the community.*

He had the bluest eyes. And it was as if he could tell what any one person was thinking and speak aloud a confirmation that they were not alone in the feeling. Even the female scientists let out a giggle in his presence. Even the General said he was *A genius, a real genius!* We watched him ride through the desert on horseback, we watched him seemingly unaffected by strong martinis and chain-smoking. He seemed unfailingly in control of himself, but not as if it took effort. We suspected he had secrets deeper than the Hill's shared secrets. Which made him — to some of us — quite tempting.

LETTERS

When the children were at school we sat at our desk typing letters to our mothers. *Bobby does the darndest things! Frank keeps busy at work. We girls have a knitting circle now.* We edited out our fear, anger, and loneliness for our mothers, who had sons overseas, who were anxious enough.

Our mothers wrote to us and said they were enclosing chocolate-covered raisins and when their letters arrived without the raisins we assumed the censors, which were other wives just like us, or maybe the WACs, had eaten them.

Our parents wrote to us and asked, *What is it like there? When can we visit? When are you coming home?* And we replied, *Soon, I hope,* or, *I don't know,* or, *We are in the West. The weather is fine!* Or we did not reply because we did not know what to say, really.

And our brothers wrote us letters that arrived with postmarks from two months prior. Our brothers described the first time they shot

112

and killed a man and the pistol they kept as a souvenir. Our brothers said: *It is odd how hard one becomes after a little bit of this stuff, but it gets to be more like killing mad dogs than people.* We replied with sympathetic sentences — *I cannot imagine what you are going through over there* — we replied with suggestions they could not possibly agree to — *Take care of yourself. Be safe.* We signed our names as we always did — *With Love, Sis*, or with more formality — *Fondly, Dottie McDougal*. Mostly, we could not understand what our brothers were experiencing because we had never experienced it ourselves, just as, perhaps, they could not understand us.

HEAT

The hot irritations of summer arrived and our husbands said we talked too much. They accused us of asking questions that were too obvious, or too personal. Secrecy, like cocktails, like smoking, like wearing overalls, was the new habit we acquired.

The summer's weather of blue skies and fast, roaring downpours paralleled our annoyance about petty things. The town was growing and there were not enough supplies for all of us. The unrefrigerated truck that carried our milk for hundreds of miles delivered it warm and nearly spoiled each week. Someone stole metal from the Tech Area and now all of our cars were subject to searches. MPs made us and our children stand on the side of the dirt road in direct sunlight as they lifted up and inspected each floor mat, as well as the trunk. *What would I want with scrap metal?* we asked them. They raised the mat behind the driver's seat and did find one thing: a soggy animal cracker smashed into the floorboard.

One Friday night at the Lodge Katherine said, while pouring us each a vodka punch, *Have you noticed Starla's outfit, ladies? Why, that's her best dress, isn't it.* Her last remark was not a question. We let the suggestion settle, except Helen, who wanted to show she'd noticed it first, added, *Those silk hose.* Was Starla wearing her best-looking outfit, a green dress and her one pair of silk hose, to get the attention of someone? Her husband, Henry, who was kind, but in truth, one of the least exceptional of our men, was out in the canyon testing something for the weekend. Her daughter, Charlotte, was sleeping over at Louise's. *Girls*, Katherine said, *think of what this might mean.* Margaret, always one to identify with sadness, replied: *Poor Henry. Poor Louise!* the group of us called out.

But what could we do?

Was their marriage not weathering well? Lisa disagreed, which was to be expected. She was, after all, Starla's close friend from Chicago. How could she not?

We sometimes resented how our husbands asked us to step out of the room in our own house so they could talk to their friends late into the night. And some of us spied and heard things, and some of us would never eavesdrop though we really, really wanted to, and some of us did not even think to listen to what our husbands and their friends were talking about because we were too busy thinking about our own worries: what Shirley meant when she said that thing yesterday, how to stretch the ration coupons to make a nice dinner tomorrow.

We watched Starla throughout the night — one eye on our husbands speaking sciencese, and one on her. Though many men gave her a glance, if she had a preference she did not show it. Each man was greeted kindly, each stance was taken judiciously. Until it was the end of the night, until it was Frank who touched her arm and her eyes betrayed her best look of neutrality.

Sometimes our husbands returned from the Tech Area and said they could not stand it anymore. We did not know if *it* was us or here or their work, but we were concerned it was us. We could not talk to our best friends about this suspicion, because they were back in Idaho, or in New York. A couple of us said, *I can't take this, either*, and actually left. We returned to our mothers. We became Nevadans and moved to Reno for a quick divorce. And our husbands moved into the singles dorms and we were unofficially, or officially, separated.

The Hamburger! Ingrid called, raising her arms, *the hamburger!* And we recalled that image of her: Starla's hamburger keeping us smiling the length of her conversation with the Director, or Starla's hamburger making us anxious because we could find no subtle way to tell her about it.

When the song ended she came over to us flushed, out of breath, she grabbed our arms and urged us on the dance floor with her. She insisted on taking the lead. Two women — we thought, *This is silly!* But we let ourselves be pulled into the middle of the room.

An arm brushing our arm, the stirring of winter desires — perhaps we spoke of Starla to soothe ourselves. After three songs we collected our husbands, who had fallen asleep in a corner chair.

HUSBANDS

We learned to accept their distracted air, their unwillingness to tell us more about their research, their ignorance of what we did all day or what we gave up to be here.

Some of our husbands sounded important and acted important and we treated them as if they were important to the project, but we would find out later that they were not very important at all. Or they were important but they never suggested they were. Some of us thought it wouldn't end for years, that we would live here until we died; others believed we would go home any day now. A few of our husbands would confirm or deny our hunches. We did not know how much our husbands knew or were keeping from us. They were physicists, this we did know, and therefore we had our own suspicions. Arthur, a single male scientist, got a beagle and named him Gadget and said he was our mascot and there was something illicit in the way he said the dog's name at first, as if he knew he was being mischievous.

One older scientist spoke only in a whisper, and then only when spoken to directly, and never made eye contact. We called him Mr. Baker, and if we knew him from before Los Alamos, back at Chicago, say, or in New York, we called him Uncle Nick, because though it was strictly forbidden to say aloud that he was the infamous, talented physicist Neils Bohr, we just could not bring ourselves to call him Mr. Baker. We admired how he played a comb covered in tissue paper. Our husbands regarded him with deference and held their tongues the moment his lips parted.

We took to reading war history books we checked out from the tiny library Helen ran. We asked ourselves, again and again, what were the options with the Army involved? We thought chemical weapons, maybe an expansion of mustard gas. We thought — we hoped — our husbands were working on code breaking, but our husbands were physicists and we had to consider what they might be able to build using their skills. We considered a weapon. We learned more than we wanted to about mustard gas — large blisters filled with yellow fluid, burning skin, blinding until death. Though we wanted the war to end, and we wanted to go home, and we generally were not skeptical, and we thought maybe it was a good war, we did not respond well to the individual stories of other people suffering from these weapons. We sometimes hoped our husbands would fail.

THE BEACH

In early June, the news came to us first through the military radio station, and when we heard it, we could not believe it. In over eight centuries, no one had ever successfully crossed the English Channel in battle. But now the military had. It seemed so unlikely, or it seemed just about time, and this was one of the few instances when we clinked our glasses with the military men and WACs, united in our shared victory.

While we boiled oats for breakfast, twenty-five thousand men — our brothers, nephews, childhood crushes — were ascending the foggy beaches of Normandy. The German Field Marshal had taken the weekend off, concluding that the high seas would make it impossible for the Allies to land and the low clouds would prevent aircraft from finding their targets. Also, and we loved this fact, it was his wife's birthday.

Every month we admired the full moon, how it lit our way back to our homes after dinner parties. Across the world others were appreciating the full moon for how it lit their ships' paths in the early dawn. We came home in a good mood — the moon did this — thinking of how small we were, how large the world was.

Now Sword, Juno, Gold, Omaha, and Utah beaches were stormed; bridges were bombed; Allies were moving forward on one front, but they seemed to be losing ground in the Pacific. Each night as we slept, other lives were ending.

WANTED

At the mail counter, where we stood asking if our mail had arrived, depositing new letters addressed to our mothers, there was a poster. What caught our eye was the word *WANTED!* We looked closer. We saw a dark-haired, pale-faced woman, her hair in a victory roll, like ours. She appeared menacing with the dark background and the direct eye contact, except her face seemed gentle, too. *Was there a killer in our midst?* She looked like one of us, but no one we exactly recognized. We studied the poster more closely and saw the writing above her head: *WANTED! FOR MURDER.* And below her neck: *HER CARELESS TALK COSTS LIVES.*

Some of us shivered, some of us got paranoid about what we told Judy the day before, some of us laughed on the inside but not the outside, for we had made the mistake of laughing at this kind of thing in front of WACs before. It did not ingratiate ourselves to them, and we needed them to obtain passes to Santa Fe and to find out how our children were doing in gym class. So we looked back, kept quiet, took our mail, said, *Thank you*, and walked home.

THE COMMISSARY

Because what we were doing was important, our commissary stocked chocolate bars. Mr. Gonzalez tended the vegetables with his watering can, but there was nothing he could do to perk up the wilted lettuce, peppers, and cucumbers shriveled in wood crates. Wrinkled zucchini, molding tomatoes, old garlic sprouting green tails. There were gallons of mustard and mayonnaise without a crisp vegetable in view. Milk in a small chest next to the vegetable bins, growing sour, and never enough for all of us. These Army-issued perishables traveled from El Paso and were not made fresher by the 360-mile journey.

We argued that there were perfectly fresh vegetables growing in the valley, so why could we not eat those instead? It was senseless, and we never got a straight answer, which was how things functioned in Sha-La. We bought cans of unmarked food and were surprised by their contents — beans, stewed tomatoes — and that occasionally — or frequently, depending on the storyteller — the cans had worms in them.

It was also at the commissary that we found new sources of information. We could tell, by their dress and stockings, who had just arrived to town. We offered to show them around the Hill and we offered to watch their children and we hoped they would lend us that pink dress we admired and share with us the tea they brought with them from London, and we hoped they would invite us over to their place to listen to new records. We traded our extra linoleum and our second pair of blue jeans for sugar, nylons, and secrets.

We budgeted ration coupons and saved up for steak on our anniversary, on our husbands' birthdays, and on the night we announced we were pregnant. Not all of us were good about rationing, and not all of us thought the rules should apply to us. We became tricksters out of perceived need, or because we wanted a bit more excitement. When our ration books were empty we wore red lipstick to the commissary; we leaned in to the butcher counter and said to the GI behind it, *You wouldn't let me starve, would you, John?* And John could rarely say no to us, women asking sweetly for meat, and we reached our arms out to receive steaks wrapped in brown paper, and we slipped him something expensive, but easier to come by: a paper bag of whiskey.

ANTS

In June, on picnics, on hikes, our children saw columns of ants in the sky. *Ants fly?* they asked. We thought of when we were younger, when we were more romantic, when we learned about the behavior of ants. We knew a lot about the mating rituals of ants because we had written a thesis on them, because our mothers had, because we remembered things Mister Smith told us in Bio 101.

We told our children this was their nuptial flight. We told them it was how ants make children. We did not say starlings hover nearby, watching, waiting until the ants are too tired to fight, or too dizzy from the day, and all the starlings have to do is open their mouths to receive this humming column of food in the sky.

From afar it looked like falling rain and we did not tell our children how the male ants beat their wings excitedly, mount, and drop in hundreds from the sky. How the queen flies away, tears off her own wings, digs a hole, forms a nest, and waits for her children to hatch.

We let them make an anthill from a Mason jar and keep it in their room. They fed the ants breadcrumbs and within a few days the ants died. While our children were away at school we dug up new ants and replaced the old ones, so for at least a little while our children would not know there are things they cannot save.

THE THEATER

Since the draft age had been extended in 1941 and our husbands were no longer working at the university, we worried they might have to leave us to fight in the war. But we were told there was no way our husbands would ever have to go to war since they were working on a war project. Sometimes the draft letter did come, and our husbands left for San Francisco, and we were certain they would be called to the Pacific theater, or we had a feeling it would all be okay.

If our husbands were drafted, or our brothers, we hated the term *theater* to describe parts of a war. If we did not have anyone in battle, or if we had generations of men in our families who had been in battle, we loved the term *theater*, and we thought it conjured both the drama and the artifice.

We heard news that the U.S. invaded the Pacific islands of Saipan, Guam, and Tinian, but thankfully, all of our husbands who were drafted returned, because they were working on a war project already, and they did not leave for the Pacific. But they were here, on the Hill, in the Tech Area, fighting anyway.

OUR CHILDREN

How much was parenting like warfare?
Digging trenches, changing diapers, gunfire,
or a child's head hitting the corner of a coffee
table — hours of boredom followed by
seconds of terror. We felt we had been lied to
about how lonely raising young children
could be, about how for the first year we were
not us, but them.

In our second pregnancy we birthed nine-
pound children that others envied. We had
lost our first and did not believe we were
actually having a baby until it was on our
chest, scooting down to find our breasts. We
ate huge piles of mashed potatoes and
meatloaf as soon as we delivered. We lost our
baby weight while we rested for ten days at
the hospital, or our stomach muscles never
recovered and our party dresses no longer fit,
but we could not afford or find the time to
make another.

When we brought home the second child, our
first child wanted to hold it, or our first child
said, *Put that back inside your belly.*

Our children had squeaky voices, were dawdlers, kicked the chairs in front of them, would not make eye contact with strangers, or else they spoke rapidly, frequently, giggled, passed notes, started rumors. They were restless. They loved that there was not enough water to wash their faces or brush their teeth. They refused to put on their galoshes. They took off all their clothes in the street and blamed their stuffed animals for their mischief. In other words, they were just like us. Or they were like our husbands, or they were just like the black sheep of our families, our uncles, and we asked, *How did this creature ever come out of me?*

We read a book about the effects of war on children that said children, during wartime or not, bite and kick one another and steal toys without regard for the other children's unhappiness. It said there was an ongoing war happening in the nursery. The outer world matches the *real aggressiveness that rages inside every child*. War is natural and therefore the effects of war on children were minimal. The authors said children arrive at shelters after their homes are destroyed and play merrily, and eat heartily, and this was proof that a 350-pound bomb does much less damage to a child than a divorce. And some

131

of us agreed and felt better about the war and felt bad for Susan, whose husband was lost in the Pacific, and some of us felt angry at Myrtle for telling her husband she wanted to separate — *Think of the children!* we exclaimed to her, rattling the pages of the book in her face, but she would not listen.

Our children were newborns, were toddlers, were in elementary school or in junior high, were teenagers or were in college and therefore forbidden from visiting us on the Hill or from even knowing where we had disappeared to. Sara and Moll's daughter would be leaving Los Alamos for college at the end of the summer and would not be allowed to come back to visit, nor could we visit her. Until the war was over. Until our work here was done. How long would that be?

A military psychiatrist came to town and asked if we wanted to have our children evaluated. We said yes because we wanted to hear from a professional how stunning our children were becoming. The psychiatrist gave them white paper and crayons and asked them to draw whatever they liked. Our children drew trains and Humpty Dumpty and the psychiatrist told us this meant that although our children seemed happy, they actually believed life was very hazardous. We frowned. We asked what we could do. But some of us thought, really, that perhaps our children were just perceptive. We could not disagree with our three-year-olds' assessment. Life was hazardous. We thanked the doctor and we started questioning our children's artwork anyway, because we were supposed to, and we asked ourselves, *Are they happy? Really happy?*

The psychiatrist said we should have taken longer to wean them. Or we needed to tell them more often how smart they were. Or *we* needed to be less anxious, and the psychiatrist suggested we make an appointment for ourselves to come back alone next Tuesday.

DAYS

There was always something to get excited about, something to do, but many of us were getting bored. A secretary called, *Fire!* over the town PA system and we came running with a tub of dirty dishwater. A man had tossed his cigarette into a puddle of oil.

We hated the barbed wire fence, although some of us hardly noticed it with time. But for a few of us the barbed wire fence was a reminder of concentration camps and we felt ill whenever it, which stretched along the border of our town, came into view.

Michael, our husband's friend whom we referred to in letters as *our dour friend who misses New York*, founded the Mushroom Society — a group that listened to Mahler recordings in the Tech Area late in the evening. And since many of us were not allowed in the Tech Area we stood outside the fence, near the north-facing windows, in the snow, to listen to the deeply serious and the utterly commonplace. The tentative measure of something slow to wake. The dark forest rumblings. Mahler's sad, beautiful, and expansive music.

Sandy's family was moving into Bathtub Row and for housewarming presents we bought her towels with our own initials embroidered on them and said, *In case you want to invite us over!*

Was Los Alamos a summer camp for adults? Some of us felt helpless at the arrival of unexpected guests, constant knocks on the door to borrow flour or to invite us to a bridge game, while others felt invigorated by it. But sometimes when our husbands tried to cajole us to go out and socialize with their friends we said, *I'm in for the night — not feeling well*, smiled, and settled back into the couch with a novel.

In many ways, life on the Hill was the same day again and again. In a closed-off community, small misunderstandings could quickly become melodrama. A couple of *surely innocent* details said to one person became a subplot worthy of Tolstoy, a subplot written and rewritten by other members of the town. If a few facts had to be overlooked for the purposes of good storytelling, they would be.

At a party at the Director's house Katherine pretended she was part of a conversation about potato casseroles but instead we watched her out of the corner of our eyes. She arranged herself to be standing alone with Henry, and we heard her ask, *How's Starla?* with concern in her voice that we were sure she did not feel. *Just fine, Katherine, just fine.* If he got her hint, he rejected it.

In August we heard news that Paris was liberated. *Paris*, we said, recalling the place fondly — the spring we studied abroad and shared a studio flat with a balcony only two could stand on, a loveseat of a balcony that looked into the attic apartments of the building across the way, where we could see, even if we did not want to, a particularly pale man who seemed to enjoy not wearing clothing. Even if we never lived there, even if we never visited, even if we knew Paris only in books, we thought we knew the café life of the 14th arrondissement, the academic life of the 5th. Paris, liberated, their motto standing true — *tossed by the waves but never sunk.* Though we loved Paris, when a parade was called that evening, only twelve people participated — suggesting how far inward we had turned, or suggesting we were tired of the Hill's alternating routine of trumpeting and nail-biting.

EXCEPTIONS

Our mothers were ill or our fathers had birthdays and we could not visit. But we learned — in a way that we never wanted to — that there was an exception. We packed our suitcases and took trains to Duluth, to Los Angeles, past the soda shop where our first loves kissed us, past the service flags and blue stars hanging in windows — we could see who had gone off to war while we were gone — and past windows where blue stars were replaced with gold. Back into our parents' houses, back into our mothers' arms, to the funeral parlors of our hometowns, where we stared into the faces of our own dead brothers.

A few of us got an exception of a different nature. Our sisters announced their sweethearts were coming home and they were getting married. Though our husband's request for both of us to travel to San Francisco for the wedding was denied, a wife was permitted to go, and we busied our summer with correspondence to our sister about color schemes, florists, and menus. It was the first time in a long time we'd thought about the outside world. Searching through boxes in the back of our closet for nice gloves and a presentable dress for the wedding brought back memories of home. We could smell the sea again. How were the neighbors we'd left behind? Was the pharmacist still frowning as he counted pills? How was the butcher? Had the weeds grown tall around our house and was someone else living there?

Our parents met us at the train station while our sisters, weak from wedding preparations, were in bed with pneumonia. Their future husbands, who had arrived from the Pacific two days earlier, were lying in their own childhood beds across town. Our first thought about our parents was, *They look tired*, or, *They look so much older*, and they probably had the same thoughts about us, too.

On the drive home we chatted but only half listened and recall little — something about the neighbors' dog, something about the tree in the front yard — but on our minds instead was the cool sea air and the familiar, cleanly designed bridges that brought out a feeling of grandeur in us as we crossed them, as if the feat of their construction was somehow ours as well.

Back in our hometowns, past the doorman, the mailman, up the stairs, inhaling the bay, the bakery, the trash in the alley, the soft light, the sound of a foghorn. And up two flights or into the elevator we went. We closed the brass gate and looked above to see the white clouds of New York through the skylight, and we arrived at our door and rang the bell just because we could. We picked up the telephone to hear the operator ask us what number we would like to reach, and we dropped our suitcases in the entryway to our bedroom and remembered what this home offered that we had not been in for years: a shining porcelain bathtub. Our mothers kept our sons and daughters occupied while we soaked until our fingers and toes wrinkled.

We found our sisters tired from their illnesses but ecstatic. They asked us for advice. We warned them of dehydration caused by nerves — *drink water constantly* — and we told them to take nothing as a sign, unless it was a good sign. On the eve of our own wedding our husbands woke with their legs as tight as statues, their veins visible like a colt's; they woke and stood and collapsed on the bed and if we thought, *Is this a sign?* we did not say it, and our husbands did not say it. Anyway, really, it was not a sign, we told our sisters, it was our anxiety, it was dehydration. Drink more water than you think possible.

CLOSE QUARTERS

We were tired of borrowing Jane's green dress, even though we told one another, *It's not the size of the wardrobe that counts, it's the shape.* We felt better about ourselves when we glanced at Ruby's sagging hemline, when we considered Annie's matron bulge.

We conspired to stop wearing decorative hats and delicate stockings because this was the new power; to have been here longer was to have more authority. And one way we had authority was by knowing the fashion of this place. We wore blue jeans and cackled over the new girls who wore heels. *Did you see her get stuck in the mud outside the post office? Poor girl. She'll never get those clean!* Or we tried to avoid this kind of talk.

We told the new arrivals — Pauline with the pink half-moon manicure that called attention to her stubby hands, Doris with the upswept victory roll, Betty with the calm voice — what was what in this town. *Those are the bathtub houses, those are the four-family houses, those are the Quonset huts, and those are the trailers.*

140

We told the new girls, *You are going to need a year's supply of lotion for just one month here.* We watched them notice the dryness and lick their lips. We thought of our own dry lips and hands when we first arrived and we thought, *Silly thing, you are only making it worse.*

We recollected how we, too, were horrified when we first arrived to see women wearing blue jeans or ski suits. How we cussed at the runs in our stockings created by brushing against a table, a piñon branch, or who knows what. How we were down to one pair of silk stockings with no way to get more. The fashion magazine *Glamour* came to Shirley in the mail and she read aloud to us: *There's no substitute for a daily bath as the groundwork of glamour!* And we all longed for a bath we could not take, and Esther said aloud what we all thought: *Oh, be quiet.* And she shut the magazine.

Our attire took on the drab camouflage of the surroundings; the beige and muted tones of the desert became our wardrobe — and we could see how this attire appeared to an outsider, to the newly arrived. There was the sunlight's skill at color and though we were subtle, though we often blended into the background, we left our red lips on one another's coffee cups and highball glasses.

Doris led the charge of wearing broomstick skirts and Indian jewelry, perhaps thinking it would endear us to the Spanish Americans and Indians. We agreed that if you were in the soup it was best to swim.

September came, and inside our duplexes and apartments we heard the sounds of other families: thuds, bedsprings, a pattern of toy trucks being thumped on the floor, the rhythm of brooms, of vacuums, of steps, of typewriter keys. We heard timers, shower curtains, radios, faucets, the scrubbing of floors, our neighbors singing along. We heard the especially painful wails of children who were not our own.

On our neighbors' radios, which wafted into our living rooms, inescapable, we heard the weather interrupted to report, instead, that U.S. forces had landed in the Philippines. These were routine interruptions, almost as regular as Bob Hope ending every show with *Bye-bye, and buy bonds.*

If we joined the square dance group we made squaw costumes and wore heavy Indian jewelry. The colors of our husband's badges were forgotten then, and we said it was the most inclusive place on the Hill, our square dance group, and we did not think about how those of us in this group were all Catholic. And no trailer mothers wanted or found time to lead the Cub Scouts, and so their boys were discouraged by some of us from joining the Cub Scouts. Nevertheless, Carol arranged for a sandbox and swing set to get their children out of the streets and a Quonset hut with a Ping-Pong table and a Victrola for the teenagers. We led the City Council and won the battle to keep our spare-room apartments as well as the fight not to expand the firing range.

Perhaps the WACs thought we were prima donnas. Cecilia said they resented being told they were going to an island but had to come here instead. When we asked for carpet in the bedroom they narrowed their eyes as if to say our lodging was already too luxurious. *If you want it you'll have to buy it and install it yourself.*

We did not like taking orders from girls in khaki. We especially did not like WACs slamming their cash registers shut and shouting, *You'll have to get in another line.* We were sure they did not want to be running the cash register at the commissary, but they had signed up for it, not us.

And we thought the WACs who assigned our homes and our maids picked favorites, and we said we were snubbed by the WACs when, upon giving birth to a second child, we were placed in a home next door to a single scientist who practiced his trumpet each night.

Some of us had the rare ability to project nonchalance, and some of us had the talent of spontaneity, and many of us knew how to give meaningful compliments. Some of us were said to be judgmental, and some us were called cynical by our husbands when we speculated about how the war would end. A few of us had the curse of truthfulness, which gave us little power.

No matter how alone we felt there were things we could never do as individuals. A woman cannot conspire with herself. Alone, we were not a pack, a choir, or a brigade. But together, we were a mob of women armed with baby bottles and canned goods, demanding a larger commissary, and we got it. We were more than *I*, we were *Us*. We were

Us despite our desire for singularity. We were the *Us* that organized the town council and nominated Starla to speak for the group. Katherine had wanted the role, we knew, and as much as we appreciated her entertaining stories, we realized, upon considering her for the role, we did not completely trust her.

As the one most capable of spreading rumors, Katherine was possibly the most indiscreet. And what if her ecstatic utterances did not just sing out to the ears of the town but were also muffled into thick sheets spread over pine needles, lost between the tangle of brush and branches? There was no one else as adroit as Katherine, no one else better at prying without it seeming so and at providing evidence of those suspected of playing Musical Beds. Her loud voice should have given rise to other suspicions, but when we were in her company, we thought more of what she told us and less of what to think about her own marriage. Which is to say, some of us now suspected we had been misled.

Our childhoods were similar. Our childhoods were similar in the way that our parents were distant, or our childhoods were similar because our parents always thought we could do better, or our childhoods were similar because we wrote our mothers twice a week and we all wished we were back in Omaha. We were from a European country and we all did not understand why Americans announced, at dinner parties, that they were going to the bathroom.

Though we became friends quickly, for the most part we still kept things from one another. We told Mary that we felt we were incapable mothers and we told Wendy about the ongoing flirtation with Donald *which is of course nothing!* because these two friends were both shy and never talked to the others. Or late one night we confessed to Susan, which we immediately regretted, and when we saw her at the Director's party the next day we blushed because she knew something real about us that we were actually ashamed of, and could we trust her? We told no one that we hated the family we had left in Des Moines, that we never wrote them and hoped they thought us dead, or that we felt bad about the way we had treated them now that we were untraceable, in a town that was not on the map, with our real names stricken from the record, for all this time. Or we decided to write to our family. To apologize. Because the censors, our friends, would read our letters, instead of saying we were sorry, we told our family how much we missed them, how we looked forward to talking with them when we could come home, how we'd say more later.

EXCURSIONS

When we wanted to leave we were finger-printed, and even then we could only go as far as Santa Fe. We were told, for the millionth time, secrecy was imperative. We were given pamphlets that said we were *not to mention the topographical details that are essential to the Project*. But because we did not know what the project was we did not know what was essential. Were the pine trees essential? The sunsets? The mud? When we traveled to Santa Fe we said as little as possible and felt painfully self-conscious.

The journey was rickety and we hated it, or it was thankfully long and we loved flirting with the GI who drove the bus. We wanted to go to the Indian market in Santa Fe, but some of us were afraid of contracting polio, though it never came to Los Alamos. Or at least we mostly recollect that, though Alice reminds us that the high school science teaching schedule had to be revisited when Cecilia, the wife of a young chemist and science teacher, developed some kind of polio and died. It was a shocking event for everyone, and now, oh yes, we remember, that's right, that was quite awful.

We were told to talk to no one, to instead just nod and smile. We came down from the hill with our scraggly children, and we were instructed to be only one thing: *unfriendly*. When asked where we were from we all gave the same address: Box 1663, Santa Fe. We told our children to lie. About what town they lived in, about what their name was. *You are Donna, you are William*, we would tell them. *You are just passing through; you are visiting from Texas*. When asked what was being built up there on the Hill we instructed our children to say, *Windshield wipers for submarines*. And when they did say this, the shopkeepers said, *She's a smart one!* and smiled. The shop owners would see our children the next month, and the next, and each time our children would look down at the ground for their lies uncovered, or our children would tell other lies to cover the first ones.

And occasionally, on the sidewalks in Santa Fe, we ran into friends from our college days and we panicked. When they asked us to have a Coke with them we said yes and when they asked, *How are you doing?* and, *What are you doing here?* we stiffened and looked around and fumbled. We saw young men in snap-brim hats study us from store windows, and we felt their eyes on us, but when we looked back to see them again, they were gone.

WAVERLEY

In the autumn, when the aspens turned the mountains into multitudes of gold, we took walks alone. Although when we first arrived we thought hiking was boring, later we wanted to see all of the mountaintops. On the highest slopes, the small leaves of the aspens quaked. And we listened to them — they were such exposed things holding on and making vulnerable, fluttering music — and this quaking gave us a peaceful feeling. We stood there thinking of nothing except leaves, leaves, leaves.

Or standing in this grove brought out the melancholy in us, and we felt a rush of sadness, in our throats, in our stomachs, in our necks, but it, too, was not attached to any one thing in particular. It was just this, the aspen leaves, not falling, but making the sound of holding on.

We walked back home. We had a secret. We set the table and laid out the steak we had saved our rations for and sat down. But before the first bite, we announced, *I'm pregnant!* Leon smiled and got up and kissed us and looked at us, really looked at us in the eye for what felt like the first time in months or Sam got up and felt the table. And we said, *What should we name him?* We hoped it was a him and we had science backgrounds so we thought it would be funny to suggest first names that were elements from the periodic table and we said, *Uranium Fisher,* and before we could say more our husbands put their hands over our mouths. We asked, through voices muffled by their hands, *What's wrong?*

Someone will hear you. Keep quiet. They sat back down and stared at us. Somewhere the dry leaves were falling.

CHILDREN

We said we had four children including our husbands.

There was a small body of water, a man-made pond, in the center of town, which our children used to ice skate on during the winter and swim in during the summer. They dug holes under the fences, stole wood from construction sites, and built forts on the other side. They climbed in and out of the barbed wire fence through a hole covered by a woodpile. We thought woodpiles were snake dens and we told them not to do it, but we knew they would, and we had our snake kits ready.

Mud, mud everywhere in the rainy summers, in the melting snow of spring, and our children played like piglets. Soon they carried pocketknives they got by trading candy with their friends, and we were afraid but we knew we had to let them be children. Once we found out from our neighbor that on their way to school, as they cut through backyards, our young boys slashed the underwear hanging on the clotheslines, and we took their pocketknives away.

Our Bobbies pretended to change flat tires, our Cheryls were the best skiers, our Michaels threw rocks at the garbagemen. They played Ring Around the Roses and held hands with other women's children for the first time. They bobbed for apples; they made Valentines.

Our children would be in class and hear a big boom and ask, *What was that?* Over time they grew accustomed to it and like most children were preoccupied instead with their friends, with the girl who won the spelling bee, with what they might eat for lunch, with what fort they might build after school.

The fire chief's daughter was the most popular, our daughters told us. Our daughters just wanted to be left alone, wanted to read books, or wanted to be well liked, but they were foreign, they were not the fire chief's daughter, they were outsiders because we did not go to church on Sundays.

When our daughters, the talkative ones, weren't doing well at school we met their history teacher, our friend Louise, after class. *What is she doing wrong?*

She never puts her hand up in class.

This was something we could manage. We had been that girl, or we could not understand being that girl. Either way, when we got home we marched into our daughters' rooms. *I don't care if you know the answer or not, you put up your hand.* And wouldn't you know, their grades in history improved.

Our children asked us to fix their bikes and to replace their tires so they could ride to the stables and feed and exercise the horses. And once we did fix their tires they said they would rather walk. We told one another then, *All boys should be buried at twelve and not dug up until they are eighteen.* But we thought of the boys actually buried at eighteen, and we didn't say it again.

Our children found shotgun shells they thought were empty and one child banged them against the ground; they exploded, they tore through Cadillacs, they knocked our boys back, two boys could not hear for a week.

POND

We were at our children's piano lesson when Sarah came running in to say Patrick was in the pond but not moving. The pond our children ice-skated on, the pond our children swam in.

Over the mud hill, in our galoshes, in our untied oxfords, we ran. Starla leading, Margaret losing her left shoe. Folded in a green wool blanket next to the pond, Ingrid was bundling him, shooing away anyone who came too close. She swayed and rocked his long body as if he were still an infant. Kissed his forehead, his cheeks. It was, as we knew it would be, too late.

We went to her. If there were a thing to say we would say it, but there was nothing. *I'm sorry.*

But we could stand at the side of the pond with one leg ankle deep in mud and hold her until her sobbing momentarily stopped, until an MP or hospital orderly took Patrick away. Blissful-heart, breaking hours, frail body, fainting body, we could never change what time, too, can't: your own child, gone. We stood and we tried to tell her with our standing: she would survive.

At home, we brought out the vacuum, though we had just cleaned the carpet that morning. Under the loud hum of the machine, where our neighbors could not hear us, we sobbed.

LONGING

Because our husbands were hard to reach, and dinner was the only time we saw them, we planned lively tales to get their attention, which were usually dramatic retellings of the mundane activities of our days. Oscar got into the trash again, Maria had to be told twice to get the floor clean, Bobby threw a tantrum at the commissary. Occasionally our husbands had not heard the news, and we reported on war updates we got from the radio, or from the GIs.

Or perhaps we let silence shade the evening, and we felt that we were a portrait on the wall, more invisible the longer it had been in its location, and we felt we were no longer new, no longer different, no longer eye catching. We raised our pitch; we made our tone pretty and light. It was no use. We wanted a night out with our husbands, we wanted to be anonymous for a few hours, we wanted to flirt. We missed brushing off the men in line at the deli counter. Crocuses pushed up through the hard clay, and we longed to be longed for.

Some of us did not want to acknowledge our longings, for what that might mean, for how we were weak to them. Others of us were more confident, were better fantasizers, could desire a piece of chocolate but could go without it — and so we announced, at dinner parties, in front of our husbands, *Frank, my dear, I could eat you up.*

At home, when we wanted a diversion, when we wanted sensory stimulation, when we wanted exercise, when we wanted social interaction — perhaps we went shopping. Because we were frequent browsers we were confident in what we liked and we were rarely talked into buying expensive and ugly things and therefore we did not feel any remorse. But for some of us, if we did buy anything, or if we checked our watches and noticed, to our surprise, three hours had gone by and we still needed to think about dinner, we did not feel elation, but a heaviness, a guilt for what we did with our time. Sometimes we returned home with items we did not previously plan to purchase — houndstooth slacks — and these sorry items stayed in our closet, first in the front and then to the back — with the tags on, until finally, accepting our bad purchase, we donated the neglected item to charity.

On the mesa, when we felt restless, sleepy, antsy, distressed, and bored we went to the commissary, which did not console us at all.

SPREADING RUMORS

People were talking; it was our job to spread a fantastical rumor to confuse any spies and nosy neighbors. In Santa Fe they could see our columns of smoke during the day and our lights at night. And on occasion the sleepy town was overtaken with women who had confident strides, who bought up the town's supplies of purses, children's shoes, and spare parts for washing machines.

So the Director told us to go to Santa Fe and pretend we were tipsy. We were ordered to hide our wedding rings in our pocketbooks and lean into the ears of local men, to dance slowly with them until they wanted to hear what we had to share. We were instructed to say we wanted to tell them a secret. We asked in a voice we tried to make deeper, *Do you ever wonder what we are doing up there?* We were told to say we were building an electronic rocket ship. But these local men in cowboy boots were tipsy, too (we did more than pretend), and they wanted to tell us their secrets instead. They wanted to tell us their dreams for their future or what they had lost so far: *I want to own a ranch. My ex-wife is good with the children. I didn't mean to do it. I'm gonna get her back. And my kids. You'll see.*

We were bored with these men, or we were intrigued, or we wanted to hear anything except their sad longings, which did not include us. We liked having our wedding rings in our pocketbooks for a couple of hours and we liked pretending, at least briefly, we were single. The men came in close — we could smell their aftershave, could feel their warm breath. We said to ourselves, *It's for the war effort,* and twirled our way across the dance floor.

CROSSROADS

Fall passed quietly but winter did not: 1944 was ending and the Allied troops were preparing to advance into Germany. Our maids came in the morning and told us their boys in France and the Pacific wrote letters that said they felt walled in by the jungle, that their ship would soon sail, that their destroyer had seen action and they were doing just fine.

And one day we heard that the Germans attacked in Belgium near Malmédy and Allied communication was cut. We wrote home inquiring about our friends, our brothers, and our cousins, as we often did when the news became too much. More updates came: that Germans dressed in Allied uniforms drove U.S. tanks, using white tape to falsely indicate minefields, which cut off roadways. An American troop, weak from the cold, took off their weapons and raised their hands to the sky. German troops told them to stand in a field near the crossroads, and shot the unarmed prisoners. We heard of prison camps, of people being underfed, killed, and used for scientific research. We thought, *dirty Axis*.

There was this, and another fight on the other side of the world, in the Pacific, where Japan was occupying large sections of southern China. U.S. air forces were bombing Iwo Jima. We'd hear these things, feel rushes of emotion, or feel it was fairly normal at this point, and life resumed. A notice in bold to conserve water, a flyer for the latest movie, and the drama of the garbage collectors versus the neighborhood dogs.

On our walk back from the commissary on Christmas Eve we saw our husband's friend Robert packing two green suitcases and a canvas bag into an Army car. *Robert,* we called. *Where you headed?* It was possible he could be going anywhere — someplace he could not tell us — but this was not a weekend bag, this was, perhaps, all he owned. *Home,* he said. We gave him a look. He said he was worried about his wife whom he had left behind in Poland. But as he said this he did not look at us. Something seemed odd — was it possible he was lying? He had not told us of his departure earlier and this seemed to be quite sudden, but we wished him a safe trip. We relayed the news to our husbands that evening, who seemed surprisingly unsurprised.

PARENTING

We toilet-trained our children and felt good because we were doing something we could somewhat control. Our children got sick and we wondered how much their illnesses were caused by our own anxiety, as the psychiatrist had suggested. We fretted over their eating habits, and we took them to the hospital, and we were laughed at by Army doctors who said everything was normal. But we still felt something was wrong, though in most cases their appetites came back.

We thought some mothers were better than we were: some mothers could get their children to eat more of their dinner, some mothers could suggest that their children pick up their toys and make it seem as if the children had thought of the idea on their own and their children ran to put their toys away, and their homes were clean.

Our children drew us in purple skirts, in blue overalls, with orange glasses. They drew us in the backyard hanging laundry, in the kitchen with a highball glass, in front of the house holding their hands, with red flowers as tall as we were, red flowers that never existed in the front yard. They drew their fathers less frequently and we sometimes had to remind them to include their fathers in the drawing. But they never left out the neighborhood mutt that got into the trash and spread our dirty tissues across the lawn.

Our husbands brought home plastic objects in primary colors and we did not know that they were casings from parts of the Gadget. We saw them in a box and gave them to the children to play with, or we made Christmas ornaments out of them and proudly showed our husbands the colorful tree, and our own inventiveness. Our husbands stood stiffly and grimaced and asked us to take them down immediately.

With our children, our husbands used their belts often, or sometimes, or they would never think of such a thing after what their fathers had put them through. But they did, on occasion. Or their fathers had been gentle, had taken deep breaths when they felt most frustrated, and so they did that, too; our husbands, who did not spend as much time with the children as we did, were far more patient than we were.

Our husbands made meatloaf and we praised them profusely. Or they did the dishes, or they neither cooked nor cleaned. Some of our husbands were exhaustively tender: they listened as our daughters named every tree they passed, *Maria, Theodore,* and told their stories. *That one has a twin brother and he hates all the noise. We should be very quiet now when we walk by him.* We loved the first wrinkles that formed around our husbands' eyes and we admired them as they carried our children to bed.

Our children butted heads and brought home lice. Our children got the flu and chicken pox but, thankfully, never polio, which was one of our biggest fears. An iron lung would not make the trip up these hills even if we could afford its price tag: the cost of a new home. Our children gave the Director chicken pox and until he was rid of it he went unshaven and grew a scrawny beard.

We had chubby children we tried to put on diets, feeding them broccoli and American cheese and corn and canned peaches and *No more seconds!* and *Go outside and play!* but they remained plump and we thought it was in order to defy us. Many times, we were right and many times, we were wrong.

Time moved slowly — but the notches on our children's closet doors indicated that time was in fact passing, as did the war updates: Hitler had ordered a retreat on the Western front, having run out of fuel to keep the tanks going, and no one nearby was willing to give him any. To many of us this seemed particularly humorous.

One afternoon, a man in a snap-brimmed hat knocked on our door and asked if he could come in. Once inside, he told us that the neighbor girls were playing in the front yard of the apartment across the street when a man tried to coax one to come with him behind a toolshed. One girl ran for her mother, but by the time the mother got there, the man was gone. Had we seen anything? We reached for our sewing basket. Earlier that day, when we retrieved our clothes hanging on the line we noticed that our own underwear were slashed. We handed them to the man in the snap-brimmed hat. He held them up, inspecting. *I'd just thought it was the neighbor boys that cut through the yard.* After contemplating our panties for what felt like far too long, he replied, *No pocketknife did this. Please don't repair them. We may need them as evidence*, and handed them back to us. The man said the matter was not

168

to be discussed so as to avoid causing panic in the town. We thought of some girls who might not run home to tell their mothers. Some girls obeyed all kinds of commands, not just ours. And when he left we gazed out our window, watching the sunlight reflect off the snowy hillside. We got up and took our revolvers down from the shoebox in the closet. Or we got up and put our son's baseball bat by the sofa. We locked the door for the first time.

Other times we were angry at our children for distracting us from letter writing, from dinner, from our own thoughts. Sometimes we were angry at our children for paying no attention to us, for rolling their eyes, for locking themselves in their messy rooms. We had hoped it was our parents that were the problem with our own youthful detachments, not us, but our children were showing us the truth. They pulled away when we tried to kiss them and yet they still cried quite easily. Their smiles turned to smirks and they learned to talk out of the side of their mouths. We grew nervous in their presence and felt prepared for them to mock us at any time. We tried to reduce our children to something manageable in our minds, not what they were, exactly, but something different, simpler.

There was never any quiet; our bathroom doors did not lock, our children came in asking, *When am I going to be old enough to carry someone on my back?* And *When can I climb on the roof?* And *When can we go see Grandma?* And the older ones asked: *Why can't I stay at Madeline's tonight? Why can't I go to the dance? When can I shave my legs? What is Dad working on?*

Our boys started growing tall and saying *No* and meaning it. They were bored, too, but differently.

Our children talked back to us in Spanish slang they learned from the carpenter's children, or the Tewa they learned from our maids and we did not understand, though we were pretty sure we were being insulted.

We hosted parties for the teenagers of the town, mostly the children of other people — the carpenters, the cooks — and we taught the boys to dance as a way, we thought, to keep them out of trouble. And if our own sons and daughters weren't teenagers they began the dance of hitting and punching one another, no longer knowing what to do with their affections — their bodies growing into shapes foreign to them. Their voices, when they addressed us, were frequently close to shouting.

Some of us were older and had boys who did not smile, and they wanted to be kissed, but not by us, and there were only ten girls in their class to choose from, they said, because the Mexican girls, black girls, and Indian girls did not count. Some of us disagreed. But many girls were not interested in our boys; instead, they folded their skirts over at the waist to make the hem shorter for when a soldier walked by, and they tried out new smiles they learned about in our women's magazines. A few of our daughters didn't seem to be thinking about these things at all and instead brought home posters that said WIPE THAT JAP OFF THE MAP and when we asked where they got it our daughters said, *The post office gave it to me*, and they taped it to the ceilings above their beds.

BLAME

We were washing dishes and we saw the overflowing trash can, or a child came in asking for milk, and we were reminded of something significant: we could never be separated from our children or our husbands, entirely. At times we heard the rise of our husbands' voices lovingly in our heads, when they were away at the Tech Area for what felt like weeks, coming home only to eat dinner, and we felt as if we were widows. We would be alone hanging curtains and look back at our well-sewn, well-hung yellow drapes and hear them say, *You're an ace, Mary*, and recall fondly, or sadly, their voices.

There were other problems. Some of our husbands would not let us sleep until we made love, and we were tired but it was easier to turn toward them than to feign sleeping, so we turned toward them. Sometimes in those moments we left our bodies for a few minutes, making love as if we were in another room, and we watched ourselves, distantly, and then they snored, and then, finally, we got some sleep.

Or our husbands still came up behind us in the kitchen and delighted us with their bodies and we turned around. Our children were in bed, were outside playing, were staying the night at a friend's house. We pushed into our husbands, we pulled them in, we moved their hands up our skirts.

Or we became more like roommates or friends than lovers. We cuddled, and that was all. Or we did all of the above, at different intervals, in different arrangements, for years.

On weekends we would take hikes with them. They talked and talked about the war and Germany but their voices were sometimes lost in the rush of the river. We enjoyed nature's sounds taking over theirs, and we let them talk, and saved our own breath for the ascent back up the canyon. Sometimes between the canyon walls, we made echoes of our own raised voices. *You always. I never. I can't believe. You. You. You.* Perhaps we were frustrated by the heat, were dehydrated, or were tired; we blamed our fight on the wind or the water, on a bad night's sleep, on our frustration with the children. But it was this: *We could not leave.* Or it was this: *We feared the enemy was getting closer.*

INSTRUCTIONS

A few of our husbands read *How to Win Friends and Influence People* and offered to pay us a dime for every time they broke one of the rules, such as *Never tell someone they are wrong directly*, and *Start with questions to which the other person will answer yes*. We said we did not want to help because we did not want this persuasion directed at us. Although maybe there were things to appreciate: *Don't criticize* and *Pay little attentions*.

Sometimes spending time with our husbands and one another brought out the worst in us. And occasionally the best. From time to time we said *Why certainly* and we felt *Of course not*. Sometimes we felt so familiar, too familiar, and our own words frightened us when they came from our mouths, as did the actions of our hands: it is those we are closest to that we can harm the most. And occasionally, during a fight, we were quiet, and we waited out the silence until our husbands could no longer stand it.

Occasionally this technique did not work; our husbands could go without speaking, in the humming uncomfortable for days. We lost, and we showed them how we needed them more than they needed us. Some of us had parents who lived for decades at this low simmer, some of us had parents who might, on a good day, a holiday, say, or for the birth of a grandchild, finally play a loving tune on top of that hum, but they never, ever, forgot the solemn chord.

OTHER WOMEN'S CHILDREN

We heard mothers scream at their sons, we saw four-year-old boys walk out into the street and we saw fathers throw them against the house as punishment. We watched the windows shake. We saw children sobbing in front yards and hated what we saw, but we did nothing except talk about it. Our children watched this too and said, *Poor Michael*, and cried. Our children picked up new phrases from these violent observations, or from these children, such as *What's eating you?* Those parents worked with their hands, and we felt safer knowing they were not one of us. Or we thought they were like us and we felt cowardly for not doing anything.

Their children got in lots of fights. Their children were picked on, their children made wooden guns and wanted to be just like the soldiers. We did not know our children called their children *Okie* and *hillbilly*, or we did notice because, when we were angry that the garbage truck did not come all week, or that they let their children run wild, some of us said these names, too.

176

The older children were children of machinists, construction workers, and secretaries. We sensed that they missed the activities found in other towns — team sports, cheerleading, band — and we feared them and their boredom. We were anxious about the boys' fascination with all things Army; we let the girls babysit our children, hoping they would read the *New Yorkers* left lying around or explore our classical record collection. The carpenters' daughters were just as smart as our daughters, and they got scholarships to college, and they went. Or they were afraid of leaving their family, what was familiar to them, and they married GIs instead.

And when other men spanked our children for climbing on their swing sets we fumed and related the story to our husbands, who said we needed to relax. We were angry about the lack of social services, especially when our children reported dreams of *that bad man* who spanked them, because particularly then we felt helpless. The military police had been called on these men several times, but these fathers said, *No, I didn't do that*, and the MPs just went away.

We looked closer when we walked by the officers' hall in midday and saw Army men and WACs, men and women enjoying the day dancing, and part of us wanted to join them in the fun, but we could not. We worried about what our husbands would say, and we had children to take care of, and come to think of it, who was watching these women's children?

WHEN WE WOKE

Even without the holidays, there was continually a cause for celebration — the Allies beat the Axis, or we beat the Army by getting artichoke hearts stocked at the commissary, by extending the length our golf course, or by decreasing the size of the firing range. We went to parties every weekend throughout the year, sometimes not knowing exactly what was being celebrated.

At the British parties we sipped mulled wine and listened to recitations of limericks. If we were given to self-pity, we resolved it through dancing, and through liquor. We undid our top buttons and smiled brightly at the few GIs who were invited or who were not invited but came anyway, at our husbands, at one another, and we danced.

The flutter of the night felt a bit like college, when young men in starched white shirts or wrinkled cotton stood on front porches and asked us our names, or where we were from. And we replied with *Iowa* or *Sally*, common words, and felt the quiet embarrassment and excitement of what those questions might lead to.

We danced and sang along to *Hit That Jive, Jack*. We swayed to *I Left My Heart at the Stage Door Canteen*. We did not like *This Is the Army, Mr. Jones* and slowed our movements, stepped aside, asked our partners if they would be so kind as to refresh our drink.

We learned how to drink cocktails before dinner. We learned how to notice the flirtations between people; we talked about who was now sleeping with whom and, if the bedrooms were currently occupied by revelers, about Musical Beds. We were beginning to prefer the company of other women and because we spent so much time with them, we noticed more acutely when we were interrupted, when the men turned toward one another and how some women let their voices trail off. At dinner parties when our men were on one side and we were on the other we gathered around fireplaces and talked about gas shortages, water shortages, and people. *Kitty Oppenheimer always seems to have plenty of gas in her tank*, Mildred said, and Katherine added, *Enough to get her to Santa Fe and back twice a week. What is she doing down there?* And Ingrid told us, *I saw Frank pay a morning visit to Margaret's house yesterday. Saw him while I was having my coffee. He sure stayed awhile.*

When at a party late, when they insisted on dancing and stepped on our feet, when they slumped in a chair, we grasped our husbands by the hand. They asked, *Where we were going now?* and we said, *It's a surprise,* and we took their hazy eyes to bed. Sometimes we wandered into someone else's house thinking it was our own. And we saw someone reading a book on a sofa that looked like ours but wasn't, and we apologized, saying, *So sorry!* and closed the door.

We felt the freedom of living in isolation — no university president attended our parties, no department chair wife was around to observe the liberties we took with our dance moves or cocktails, and so on the weekends, fenced in as we were, we celebrated and square-danced, we let go. We often woke the next morning with no water and spent the day reeking of rum, and our lungs burned from smoking so many cigarettes. We wanted what we could many times not have: coffee, a shower.

Later, once the secret was out, the rumors that we played Musical Beds got around and when we arrived back home our aunts asked us, gravely, *Did you ever go to those parties?* And we responded, *Aunt Hilda! Don't be silly.*

1945

CITIES

When we heard Dresden was destroyed by firebombing some of us thought of the time our fathers took us to the market there, the pink heads of pigs all in a row. Or we thought about the time we toured towns by train with our parents, riding through the dense conifers of the Black Forest, arriving at a small town, a name we can't recall, watching an older man cross the street in lederhosen, just like a postcard, and how the tall mountain framed him. One shop had all the quaint cuckoo clocks in the glass storefront timed exactly, and at noon on a Monday afternoon we watched as the balcony doors of fifty tiny wooden houses opened in unison, and fifty windup birds popped out and made the same resonant *cu-ckoo*.

The buildings of Dresden we saw in the newspaper were now the skeleton constructions of stage props — only one side of a church, a bank, and city hall stood — it was a city of leaning towers with steel wires hanging down from the fifth or fifteenth story like willow branches. But also it was a city of statues appearing desperate and ominous above the rubble, including Hercules, Martin Luther, and several pairs of lions with long flowing manes.

A city, gone, and the Allies did this. We asked some of the wives, *Can you believe it? Dresden!* And some women said, *Thank goodness! They should just bomb Germany to bits; nothing else is going to stop the war.* And some women said, *Isn't it just awful.* It was times like this we found an excuse to borrow a horse and head south and down to Edith's house under the Otowi Bridge, because unlike us she moved to New Mexico years ago to avoid the pressure for success she felt in the East. We were introduced to her through the Director, who had invited us for dinner at her place: she occasionally hosted an invitation-only restaurant. Edith, and her Indian friend Tilano, who on holidays gave our children bows, arrows, and turkey feather headdresses, and for us, fireplace brooms and bundles of piñon kindling tied with red ribbon.

It was rumored she had a nervous breakdown and her parents agreed to let her go west instead of continuing to be a teacher. She read everything, was often writing in a journal, knew the names of every bird and plant we saw, kept a vibrant garden, was curious, listened as if she cared, and rarely said a bad word about anyone. She was an island of culture in the wilderness. *Tea?* she would ask us before we got off the horse, and soon we felt better.

But war news was inescapable and frequent: by late February, U.S. troops had raised their flag at the top of Mount Suribachi on Iwo Jima, where the rocky slopes were red with the blood of soldiers and civilians.

LOOKOUTS

Finally, to our joy, spring arrived. The daffodils emerged. We heard the U.S. invaded Okinawa and kamikaze pilots flew their aircrafts into Allied ships. We thought about those we'd once loved, or loved presently, who were out there somewhere floating in the ocean.

And then the news of President Roosevelt's death. It was frightening that he died before finishing his vow to end the war and we certainly were not comforted by the newscaster's report that the new president, Truman, was *very cognizant of his own shortcomings*. But the balance sheet of the Allies and the Axis in Europe looked better for our side, and in late April, Mussolini was assassinated.

Would the war in Europe be over? We grew hopeful, but not too hopeful; we did not want to be disappointed, and there was still the Pacific to think of.

Two years in the New Mexico sun had worn our faces. And even though we got caught in late afternoon thunderstorms there was also the threat of a lightning strike and the gusty winds spreading wildfires through dry grasses. On a clear day we could see billows of smoke a hundred miles away, and in the mornings the wind carried the smell of burning wood so close to us, it was as if we had had a campfire the night before.

We saw horses and coyotes, and for the group of us that rode outside the fence together, greater adventures. We saw mountain lions and snakes and once, at the top of the ridge, we saw a man with binoculars studying the buildings of our town below. One of us called, *Spy!* and he looked at us and ran. We galloped toward him into the rough rock and it proved too much for the horses. When Betty drew a revolver we all exclaimed and while we were exclaiming the man went out of view, but Betty was nonchalant and said, *I take this everywhere with me*, and put her gun back under her shirt.

We reported the incident to the Army and told everyone what happened; as far as we know he was never caught. And though we talked of who might be a spy, the real spy among us was someone we never suspected. He did not come up in our conversations, except to say he was quiet. Instead, we dined together on Sunday evenings; he seemed to enjoy playing murder mystery games and charades like the rest of us; he did not talk too much and he listened to us well beyond the limits of our husbands' patience. We thought he was just shy. He babysat our children while we went to dinner at the Director's house; he gave us new records for Christmas because we had complained we did not have enough to dance to. Our husbands described him as bright in the Lab. We had liked him very much, except for Marge who had said, *He sits in the corner at parties and doesn't laugh but has that high-pitched giggle. Gives me the chills.*

OUR OLDER CHILDREN

Many of us had no children when we arrived, or toddlers, but some of us were older, and when we arrived our children were nine and now they were eleven. Or we arrived and they were one of the few thirteen-year-olds and now they were fifteen. It was terrifying.

Our Nells played basketball in the gymnasium; our Timothys told the Army private who was also their Phys Ed teacher, when reprimanded for throwing stones, *Do you know who my dad is?* We hoped he said he didn't care. Our Jims built tree houses and hid ham radios from the guards in the woods.

We wanted our children's school to have everything: piano, horseback riding, French, physics, tennis. Or we thought they would be overindulged and we were relieved that they were learning side by side with children of carpenters, technicians, and truck drivers, and we were happy they were learning how to cut wood, make fires, and make do with one pair of boots.

Our Michaels and Lindas put Limburger cheese in the desk drawers of teachers they did not like. Our Janets refused to march as the WACs demanded. Our Betties and Jo Anns square-danced in gingham dresses across Fuller Lodge. On Friday nights they loved to go to the mess hall for steak dinners because on steak dinner nights our husbands, their fathers, who were less often coming home for dinner, would be there.

Our teenage daughters had left behind their friends and their boyfriends, our teenage daughters smiled too long at the soldiers and we warned the officers to keep an eye on their men and we warned our daughters we were watching them. Our teenage daughters read magazines that taught them how to look from under their lashes. Our teenage daughters skipped classes to kiss the soldiers, who were more protective of them than we would have imagined, and our teenage daughters felt guilty in ways we hoped they would. Our daughters knew they could not bring these soldiers home. And though they necked with the young single scientists, too, the young scientists did not take them seriously the way the soldiers did. Our daughters with their bodies in the shapes ours once were, with their defiance, with their hunger, with their longing. We took away their passes off the Hill.

Our children were mad at their fathers for telling them nothing, for disappearing into the Tech Area, and they spoke unkindly to their fathers, saying, *Hi*, or, *Nice to see ya*, without looking up, and under their breath they added, *finally*. And sometimes our husbands slammed their fists hard on the table, which shook the mashed potatoes.

Our teenagers were better than us at outfoxing the guards. They bribed the military police with beer and stole Army jeeps and some boys rolled them off the steep edges of the canyons. And even though we thought we were smart, holding on to our daughters' identification so they could not sneak off the Hill at night, we did not know that some of our teenage daughters just hid in the trunk of someone else's car and quickly they were off to Santa Fe, to Española, to someplace in the desert where they could do exactly what they wanted until daybreak.

THE HUSH

The coolness of spring turned into the sweat-beading heat of summer, and we felt the climax coming but we did not know what it would be or when it would happen. We had been here a year, some of us two, and our brothers, nephews, or cousins had been in the war four years. In April, Hitler committed suicide in a bunker beneath the rubble of Berlin. And when Germany surrendered a few days later, we were a town of parades and cowbells and cheering. Wouldn't the end of the European theater stop the work at Los Alamos?

It was quickly apparent that no, the work here was not done, and our husbands were gone for even longer hours. The anxiety we had about the war in Europe was transferred to the Pacific. We refocused our attention to the fits and starts of progress against Japan. It was all the same news practically — a little forward, a little behind. Our first nieces and nephews were born without us and our parents wrote asking if we could visit for a short vacation. The answer was always, sadly, *No*.

We felt our husbands' agitation in how they closed doors or walked across the living room. The sighs they made while opening the refrigerator, the curses they gave to the shower handles. There was nothing we could do to comfort them, and their abrupt movements caused our own necks to tighten. We had no outside network — friends from another town, family members, ladies from a water-color class — to diffuse the growing stiffness in our bodies, so we relied on one another, the other wives.

In the afternoons the temperature rose to a hundred. We became testy. It was *Hurry! Hurry! Hurry!* from the WACs in the checkout lane, at the post office, in the school yard. We all moved at a faster pace as we walked and therefore we dropped things — a breakfast plate slid from our hands and grazed our toes. Our vocabulary of curse words expanded.

One wife, Beatrice, left to visit her parents in Kansas because her husband told the General her father was dying. She told us her husband was sending her away but she did not know why — she said her father was in fine health.

When our husbands came home their eyes would meet ours but be someplace far, far away. Their voices were stern and they said, *Make me another drink*, or, *What did you do that for?* And they no longer — if we are to be honest — they no longer made love to us. We slipped off our clothes before turning off the lights, we glanced back at them over our shoulders, we pressed our breasts against their turned backs and many of them said nothing, did not even move. Or they said, *Not tonight.* We lay on our backs in the dark, embarrassed, counting our breaths, not falling asleep, worrying that they had taken a lover.

We thought about the female scientist who played the clarinet and could not sit still and whose girdle was too tight. We did not have access to hair color and we were now growing gray, but we thought it might do us good to cut back on sweets. We did not talk to our girlfriends about this. We thought of Jane, who was perpetually pregnant, who did not seem to have this problem, who arrived at our doors glowing in the morning saying, *So sorry I'm late!*

We thought of one another. Margaret with the best décolletage. Starla who had the most charm, who could make even Harold — Harold with the constant scowl — appear comfortable and happy in her company.

Or it could just be the war.

We gathered at one another's houses in the morning. We said, *Sit down, do tell.* Louise passed the sugar and said, without looking up, *Frank's been inoculated for island diseases.* We all knew the U.S. troops were in Okinawa, still fighting, somewhat unsuccessfully. We did not want our husbands to go there.

We leaned in, touched her arm, and her eyes filled with tears. We had taken to calling one another *Chiquita* following bad news, which we learned from our maids. *He's leaving tomorrow?* we said, frowning. *I don't envy you, Chiquita.* We knew something was coming. We conspired to find out what it was.

To discover who else was leaving we got close to everyone's husbands, made our voice a whisper, as if to tell these men a good story, and instead of telling them anything, we squeezed their biceps. The ones that were not going to the Pacific thought we were flirting with them and said, *Hey there!* and pinched us back. Maybe we were flirting. We told them they were strong. The husbands that were going to the Pacific winced where they were still healing from the shots. We reported this news back to the others.

Unknown things were happening. Explosions increased on the Pajarita Plateau, men were going south for three days a week, to who knows where, and some were leaving for overseas.

The military police began stopping us at night, shining flashlights into our eyes again as if it was the first day we arrived here, and not two and a half years later, as if they did not know us. *Halt! Who goes there?* they demanded. *It's just us, Willard*, we replied. They did not like us calling them by their first names just as much as we did not like them nosing around in our business, insisting on knowing our whereabouts. And as the military became stricter with us, and we complained, Ruth commented, *They are just bored babies. None of them will ever become a hero here.*

One night when we returned home from a PTA meeting our husbands told us Japan was withdrawing from China, and this must mean Japan was weakening, and we thought, *He might not go to the Pacific after all.* The wind made melancholy sounds through the tall pines and some of our husbands left anyway.

By June we heard the Japanese Army had given the Okinawans hand grenades and directed them to blow themselves up. *Could you imagine?* we asked one another. We heard of parents holding their children's hands and jumping off cliffs. As U.S. troops got closer, the suicides by Japanese soldiers and Okinawans increased. Within a few weeks the U.S. completely occupied the island.

A NIGHT PASSING

On the first weekend in July our husbands announced they were leaving us for a couple of days. They said, *I need a thermos of coffee and a bag lunch. Be home on Sunday.* When we presented them with a thermos and a turkey sandwich, instead of saying thanks and rushing out the door they stopped and looked at us. They looked us in the eyes. They raised their hand to our cheek and we felt it was damp, or it was chilled. They said, *I love you.* We scanned their faces, we asked, *What's going on?* Our question was met not with an answer, but a kiss. Their faces became blurred before us. Why were we crying? We knew somehow that they were afraid. They were walking out the door with a thermos and a bag lunch, and we did not know where they were going.

But not all of our husbands left us that weekend. A few of us, the pregnant ones, the ones, perhaps, with more sensitive or more nervous husbands, were told to pack for a camping trip. We said good-bye to Margaret and Ingrid, a bit confused about why some people were going away for the weekend and some were not. People who had left months prior for academic work returned with their families, saying they were just in town for the weekend.

A couple of our husbands took us to a spot along the river in the Sangre de Cristos to camp. We would have slept well but our husbands slept little, and in the middle of the night they sat up, as if startled, which startled us, though there was nothing startling happening outside our tent. *What is it?* we asked. And they said something, more to themselves than to us, and we could not make out the words. We said, *What are you saying, Jack?*

In the morning our husbands pulled the sleeping bag over their heads and did not want to get out of the tent until midday, until the sun trapped the heat inside the tent, and they emerged with deep sleep lines on their cheeks and sweat dripping down their chins.

We drove back to Los Alamos, eager to find out what we had missed.

Though most of our husbands left for the weekend without giving us any clues, one husband, Bernard, told his wife, as he held the front door open for a final good-bye, holding his brown bag with two ham sandwiches: *You might see something if you stay up all night.*

And Agnes was not afraid and she called a meeting. We gathered our clues. We compared notes about when our husbands came and went, pulled out the map, and tried to guess how far they had traveled and where they had gone. It seemed that all the important people had left for the weekend except us. We developed a plan: we would watch whatever it was from the porches of our houses. Whatever it was, we would experience it together.

We looked toward the Jemez Mountains in the late afternoon and again in the evening. The sky was made of watercolors: pretty, but nothing unordinary. We cooked dinner, the sun descended, we put our children to bed. We sneaked over to Agnes's, hoping our children would not wake.

Or instead we fell asleep on our children's beds with *The Brothers Grimm* in our hands. Or we were not invited over by Agnes because she did not like us, which we had considered, though we did not know what we had done wrong. Others of us did not even realize there was something to watch.

Many of us convened at midnight on Agnes's porch. The air was cold, although it was July, and this was a fact about the desert we had finally gotten used to. We huddled into one another and thought about our husbands standing hundreds of miles away, probably, with the other scientists, maybe feeling expectant, or maybe feeling scared.

It was a new moon, and as our eyes grew accustomed to the dark, the surroundings became less and less invisible. There was a chance, given the grave way they'd said good-bye to us that morning, that our husbands would never come home. We did not say this aloud. Instead, we smoked cigarettes and passed a flask, or declined one. We told jokes, we complained, we talked as if it were any day. We asked Katherine, *How do you always look so put together?* And she told us a needle, thread, cleaning fluid, a clothing brush and a good iron were her secrets. Virginia talked about her love for Ireland. Mildred made sure the whiskey went around. Evelyn wore that purple felt swagger brim hat, which was gorgeous, if a little overdressed for the occasion, and we gave her a crosswise look we hoped she could not see but later we noticed she withdrew from conversation.

Midnight, one A.M., two A.M., three A.M., four. Nothing unusual was happening in the dark sky. The wind ceased. The desert was still. Some of us found this noiselessness unsettling and filled the space with nervous laughter or commentary that stated the obvious — *It's cold out here* or *It's so quiet*. And some of us found it calming and wished Katherine would stop being so chatty; others did not pay any mind to the quiet, or the talking, and felt at ease.

At dawn, Ingrid pointed and whispered *Look!* Far off, we could see the trees on the hillside, though the sun had not risen. It looked like a flickering bulb behind the hills. *Would it stop?* The cloud our husbands had made reached the natural clouds in the dawning sky. *How far could it go?* The explosion came to our eyes but not to our ears. Those asleep near us had no idea what was happening. The land was dark before, and now it was light and we knew: our town had made something as strong and bright as the sun.

We stood holding one another. We took deep breaths. We held our breath. We yelled. We thought it was awful, or triumphant, or beautiful, or all of the above. On this place formed millions of years ago by a huge eruption, our husbands had just made their own. We could not see what you can, our husbands jittery in welding glasses, pacing, saying, *Now we're all sons of bitches.*

We celebrated by toasting our men who were not there, toasting ourselves, toasting a hopeful end to the war. And we went back home and fell asleep in our beds, without our husbands.

On Sunday they came home blind in one eye, or red-faced, as if they had stood in the sun all day. We thought they would finally tell us something but before we could ask any questions our sons or daughters interrupted by coming into the kitchen and saying, *Can I have my peanut butter sandwich now, please?*

And when we gave them their sandwich and they walked outside with it we said to our husbands, *What is it?* And our husbands said, *Let me get some rest. Then we can talk.* Or our husbands came back smiling and gave us a V for victory sign. *What have you heard?* they asked us. We told them what we suspected. They mocked our ideas but told us to keep them to ourselves, so we knew we were on to something. Or our husbands ate chicken soup and went to bed. Or our husbands came home filthy and went straight to the shower. And while they were in the shower we gathered at Harriet's. *Can't stay long, he'll want to go right to bed when he gets out, but let's have a drink in the meantime.*

We heard that the General told security officers to keep the explosion quiet from the wives. How little he knew. Harriet handed out glasses and we said what we would do when we returned home. We began to let ourselves, finally, feel the deep sorrow we had been fighting back, once we knew there was a good chance it would all be over soon. We still did not share our greatest secret, experienced by many but said to no one: how sometimes we felt deeply alone.

Cal arrived at Harriet's door and we poured him a drink and pounded him with questions. He was a son of a missionary and grew up in Japan, and he told us what the multicolored explosion looked like up close, and he told us of the heat: *A fiery eyeball . . . it grew arms, like a giant jellyfish rising from the desert. It was purple and went up and up. Made a rumbling whirl and all the mountains rumbled with it. My face was hot.*

We asked him, *How will they use it?* He said he could not say, which suggested both that he knew and that he did not know. He told us little that was useful, really, but we all still speculated about the end of the war. We went back home and nudged our husbands from sleep, and they said, *Just be patient. You'll know soon.*

Or when we asked our husband what he had seen one husband said he could not tell us objectively, because though he saw the light, he heard nothing. He had been completely absorbed in something else. This was not surprising to hear. All of his attention had been focused on tearing up little pieces of paper and watching them fall, in order to calculate something. *What something?* we asked, but he replied, ever mysteriously, *Nothing.* Though he added, a bit bragging, really, that his calculations were nearly as accurate as precision instruments. And though this method could have seemed far too simple, we were used to our husbands finding plain ways to calculate difficult things, so of course their complete focus on little scraps of paper blowing back in the wind produced correct measurements. They shared what they were proud of, although it was usually too obscurely described to guess at.

On Monday we read the *Santa Fe New Mexican*. Amid news of cattle sales, a small mining disaster, and a horse thief on the loose we saw this: *On early Sunday morning an accidental explosion at a munitions storage facility in the Alamogordo Bombing Range caused residents nearby to experience shock-waves.* Because we were at least partially inside a secret, because our husbands were involved, we had the privilege of knowing this story was a lie. The girls came to clean Monday morning and told us their relatives' homes farther south had broken windows. Some asked us if we knew what really happened. We were angry that the information we had was not the information the general public had. Or we thought it was best to maintain these kinds of secrets.

WE CHEERED, WE SHUDDERED

A week went by before Beatrice came back. *Beatrice!* we called, in unison, from our front lawns. She told the General her father had had *a miraculous recovery!* She told us that before she left her husband had given her a code phrase. And when he wrote a letter to her that included the line, *The cat cried all night when you left*, she knew it was safe for her to return to Los Alamos. And here she was.

We received letters from our brothers saying they were leaving next week for the Pacific. We hoped our husbands — and whatever they were testing — would hurry up. We told one another it would all be over soon, but of course, none of us were certain.

And one August morning while we were checking on our flowers, Eleanor peeked her head out the front door. Her hair was still up in curlers and covered with a silk scarf colored with purple lilies. She called from across the street, *Turn the news on, Barbara — it's amazing. Maybe it's all over, maybe we will all go home*, and shut the door.

Or Genevieve tapped on our window at ten thirty A.M. She shouted, though we were right in front of her: *Our stuff was dropped on Japan. Truman just announced it. Just came over the paging system in the Tech Area. That's what they must have exploded last month.* That's what she said, *Our stuff.* Any other word, like *bomb*, was more than we were ready to admit to; or any other word, like *bomb*, still felt illicit. We could say it, but we could not say it, either.

We turned on the radio and heard the newscaster, Kaltenborn — a commentator we appreciated for his consistently more detached and objective perspective — say: *The first atomic bomb . . . equal to twenty thousand tons of TNT. A population of three hundred fifty thousand people killed by one bomb. A radius of one mile vaporized.* We could hear Kaltenborn's voice quiver — it never did this — and part of us was sure we were dreaming. *This can't be real,* we said, more to ourselves than anyone else.

Our husbands who could not repair a clogged shower drain. Our husbands who miscalculated the heat loss of old windows versus the cost of new storm windows and left us cold all winter. Our husbands who could not swim

210

or drive a car, who refused to kill the moths that swarmed into our bedrooms.

For some of us, our first thought was, *It's over!* Our husbands rushed home to listen to the radio while we made lunch. Our children came out from their bedrooms and asked, *What is an atomic bomb?* We did not know for certain so we looked at our husbands and said almost as a question, *That's what your father made?* and our husbands looked at us from across the lunch table and said, *It is.*

We cheered. We shuddered. We waited. The Japanese had not surrendered.

At lunchtime a few days later, we heard a second bomb was dropped, this time over the city of Nagasaki. How many bombs would it take until Japan gave up?

We kept the radio on during dinner and one night as we ate pork chops we heard President Truman read the Japanese surrender. Emperor Hirohito told his subjects: *The enemy has begun to employ a new and most cruel bomb, the power of which to do damage is, indeed, incalculable, taking the toll of many innocent lives. Should we continue to fight, not only would it result in an ultimate collapse and obliteration of the Japanese nation, but also it would lead to the total extinction of human civilization.*

We jumped up and hugged one another and knocked over our children's glasses of milk. Instead of scraping the plates into the garbage and washing them, we opened the back door and flung them out into the dark night, and they were flying saucers crashing against the shed. A group shouted over the PA system: *The War Is Over!* We cheered too, but some of us thought privately quite the opposite. Perhaps this was a new scale of human cruelty.

Willie Higgenbotham took out his accordion and began playing, and he led the way through the unmarked, muddy streets. We made a line behind him, and people joined in, and we became a crowd of men and women and children smashing garbage cans and hooting, *Hooray!*

The chemists among us made fireworks to celebrate our victory. We had never seen our whole town so unified, so drunk, so elated, and so loud.

We went from house to house until six A.M., we drank and danced, and as day broke we returned home still glowing with the achievements of our husbands and said affections by way of insult: *You can build a bomb but you cannot fix a leaky faucet!*

The next day we gathered outside the commissary and waited our turn to read the *Santa Fe New Mexican*. The pages became rumpled and misshapen from all of the readers, and each woman's fingertips were blotted with ink, which made smudges on our cheeks. Headlines called the bomb a *Tool to End All Wars*.

From these articles we learned information about our town we did not even know ourselves, like how many families were here exactly. Six hundred and twenty, which made the total population in the thousands, and the ratio of civilians to military personnel three to one. How did they know this, one day after the second bomb was dropped, when we, who had lived here three years, did not even know these things?

We were identified on countrywide broadcasts: *At Los Alamos, high in the mountains north of Santa Fe, scientists worked to build this bomb.* And they named our husbands: *Oppenheimer, Segre, Fermi, Bohr, Bradbury,* and several others. These were our names, too. How did they know it all so quickly? Where did they get our names? How could they describe the Hill so exactly while reporting from the coast? We went from being concealed to exposed overnight.

At a town meeting, the Director stood on a wooden platform and looked out into the crowd, a group that had grown from a handful of families to over a thousand people. His pressed suit hung off the sharp edges of his shoulders, his head looked small beneath his wide-brimmed hat, and it was disarming to see him without a cigarette. He was bony, even thinner than before, though we did not think that was possible. He was as slender as a Weimaraner, but he seemed calm.

He leaned in to the microphone, and we heard his voice through the tinny speakers. He began: *I don't have anything to say that will be of an immense encouragement. The thing we made really arrived in the world with such a shattering reality and suddenness that there was no opportunity for the edges to be worn off. If you are a scientist you believe that it is good to find out how the world works; that it is good to find out what the realities are; that it is good to turn over to* mankind at large the greatest possible power to control the world and to deal with it according to its lights and its values.

We felt ashamed, we felt proud, we felt confused. He said, *One always has to worry that what people say of their motives is not adequate. We cannot forget our dependence on our fellow men.* And he said, finally, *A day may come when men and women will curse the name Los Alamos.*

He was not booed off the stage. We looked around to the faces near us and saw, by who nodded, who smiled, who looked away, who had their arms over their chest, just who shared our feelings.

The pharmacy was out of medicine for headache, sleeping, and nausea. We were pregnant and wanted something for morning sickness but the nurse said, *Sorry, Mrs. Smith, you'll have to come back next week when we get a new shipment.* We slept little and argued more with our husbands. Or we slept little because we stayed up late in bed with our husbands.

Our friends began leaving; we threw good-bye parties each week and wondered when it would be our turn. We thought the dry air and frequent sun had aged us and we worried what we would look like to our friends and family when went back to civilian life, to the college towns and cities we came from.

The British threw a final party — we ate pork pie and peach trifle, we drank red wine and giggled as everyone toasted the Queen. Though it occupied our thoughts, many of our husbands did not talk to us about the ethics or morality of what they had done.

Our husbands slept late and stayed in bed reading. We came into the bedroom at noon and told them we had bought apples, potatoes, chicken, and it was hailing. They looked up and said, *Okay*, and looked back down at the paper.

Or we remained in bed with them, talking through the night to make up for the time when we could barely speak. We learned there was a great argument about the bomb: many of our husbands had not wanted to release it where there were people, or had wanted to pretend they could not make it at all, especially after Germany surrendered. *Should we try not to succeed?* an organizing husband asked, saying there was enough time for them to join hands in asserting that the bomb was not possible to build. Another husband replied, *Just drop it on Home Island to show Russia what we can do.* Were there murmurs in the crowd? Was there a pause? The Director spoke: *Let's just finish it and give it to the UN. Leave science to scientists and politics to politicians.*

When talking to our husbands we cried, yelled, kissed, and apologized. Or we did not, because we had grown accustomed to the new silence between us, and we no longer knew how to speak to each other candidly. Our husbands said, *The world knowing the bomb exists is the best hope for peace.* We felt personally responsible and lost our appetite. Or we could finally eat.

US

Some of us felt more distant from the group; there were those of us who felt far away from the cheering and there were those of us who were happy to be a part of it. Because we disagreed with one another, over coffee, over tea, when in line at the commissary we would whisper to ourselves, *There's Esther*, and recall her saying, *Our husbands lied to us*, or, *There's Laura*, and think of her saying, *We didn't start the war, we finished it.*

We learned *tube alloy* was the code name for plutonium. On the way to Santa Fe we shouted *Plutonium! Uranium fission!* and all the other words we had not been able to say until now. Our children sang *Atomic Bomb, Atomic Bomb* to the tune of *O Christmas Tree* though it was only September. September and the Japanese had signed the final Instrument of Surrender aboard the battleship USS *Missouri*. We felt a part of something, and the guard shining the flashlight in the backseat of the car, which was once an annoyance, or a fear, had now become a comforting indication that we were home.

In the newspaper, next to the story that Mrs. Giyon was robbed of the money hidden under her pillow as she slept last Friday night and an announcement that tomato juice was taken off the ration list, were tales about our own town: *Their babies are born in a P.O. Box! They throw wild parties with lab alcohol!* We saw our own lives from an outsider's perspective, with embellishments meant to fascinate and horrify: *wild parties, lots of babies, you know what that means!* Likely due to the rush to get the stories out, there were several misspellings, even in the headlines, such as: *NOW THE STOORIES OF THE HILL CAN BE TOLD.*

We argued over what should happen next to the Hill. Some of us said, *Peace research is the only way to atone.* Some of us said, *Nuclear research is the only way to ensure peace.* And some of us said, *Nothing, absolutely nothing, should happen here. We should leave those jeeps to rust.*

We thought of each window we had once hated, breaking. We thought of the weeds growing up and consuming the barbed wire fences. *We should leave as quickly as possible,* the Director told us, and some of us agreed. *Let each home sink deep into the mud,* Katherine said. *Then, when nature has consumed the buildings, let tour guides take over.*

Some of us no longer thought our little town was an escape from a harsh modern world. Some of us no longer thought of this place as Shangri-La.

A few of our husbands returned from Japan with pictures of what had happened. We sat on the gymnasium floor or on the hay bales and watched the slides projected on the screen. The images were of barely discernible bodies. Our husbands described the people they photographed as if they were not people, but specimens: *Those that did not die instantly, if they were close enough to ground zero, did so within a few days. Here is a child's arm in the rubble. Notice the effect of radiation.* We saw permanent flat shadows where a man once sat on the steps of the Sumitomo Bank, waiting for his shift to begin. We saw skin bubbled up where a face once was. Survivors in the streets, thirsting for water, opened their mouths. The now radioactive rain streamed black down their necks. A man standing by a river cupped his left eyeball in his hand. Warblers had ignited in midflight miles away. A rose pattern burned out of a schoolgirl's blouse and made a floral tattoo on her shoulder. Had the world gone mad? We went home and held our children.

AFTER

We never in a million years thought we would find ourselves talking about a governmental report as if it was book club reading. But sure enough, within a week, we were perusing *Atomic Energy for Military Purposes: The Official Report on the Development of the Atomic Bomb Under the Auspices of the United States Government, 1940-1945*, written by Henry Smyth, chairman of the physics department at Columbia, and just released to the public. We opened it up and our eyes caught on this sentence: *The ultimate responsibility for our nation's policy rests on its citizens and they can discharge such responsibilities wisely only if they are informed*. We continued reading, although it was a very technical document that lacked the emotional stories some of us preferred, so we stopped, or we kept at it, because in there were our husbands, and what, exactly, they had done.

How could we not have known? How could we not have fully known? In retrospect, there were maybe more hints than we cared to let ourselves consider: back in Chicago, our husband's colleague told us, *Don't be afraid of becoming a widow, if your husband blows up you will, too.* We remembered the excitement in 1939 surrounding the news that a chain reaction was possible — a bottle of Chianti was passed around and signed by all of the scientists involved. Did we turn away from the clues because our questions would be met with silence? Or because in some deep way we did not want to know?

Or perhaps we knew this might happen all along, but we never wanted to admit it.

We argued Smyth's points as well as one another's. When we read, *This weapon has been created not by the devilish inspiration of some warped genius but by the arduous labor of thousands of men and women working for the safety of their country,* many of us agreed and some of us thought of ourselves, of the work we did — in the Tech Area, in the home, in the community — and we thought, *Well, yes, everyday men and women built this thing, but we had no idea what we were building.* Like many who sacrifice something, we felt loyalty toward the outcome. We know how it can sound: how awful that we did not think of the repercussions. But we were not living in hindsight. What many of us saw, and what our husbands saw, was this: what they had been working on for three or more years had worked. It was a relief.

Some said the report shared too much about how the bombs were made, but many of us appreciated that the military had had the foresight to have so much information ready to share as soon as the bombs were used. The report ended with a call to consider the weight of the situation.

Our husbands crowded and compressed metals until the close proximity created a surplus of energy, and that energy made grand explosions. From the splitting — fission — of uranium they created Little Boy, and from the separating of a new element, plutonium, they made Fat Man.

A few of our husbands went to Washington to tell congressmen how the bomb they made should be handled, saying that it should be given to the United Nations. They were ignored and our husbands returned, deflated or determined, and said, *The U.S. government is a bunch of idiots.*

We read newspaper articles to one another that described the areas of large cities that would be destroyed if the U.S. were to be attacked by a nuclear bomb. We said, *I'm worried for our children*, and we said, *I'm worried about what we've done*, and we said, *I'm worried about peace.*

There were bushels of letters for us now — congratulatory letters from our friends and family — sent as soon as they heard the news that we were building bombs. Letters arrived from old friends whose husbands were doing their own covert activities, too, at different locations and in different capacities — Helen's husband Max was working on something *related to that work* outside of Richland, Washington, and Joan's husband Ely was doing something in Oak Ridge, Tennessee. It had not occurred to us that we weren't the only ones in secret towns doing secret work. How silly our cryptic letters seemed now. We received cards from strangers and even one signed by the President thanking us for our contribution to the war effort. Our children took to calling the new weapon Dad's Bomb and bragged to one another about how they knew all along what was going to happen, how they were great secret-keepers.

We added to the nicknames for this place *Lost Almost* and Margaret called Los Alamos

Alas instead. Some of us thought we saved half a million lives. Some of us thought we, or our husbands, were murderers, that we had helped light a fuse that would destroy the world.

LIFTED

A knife salesman appeared at our door and we thought, *How did you get past the guard?* A man selling silk stockings got a temporary pass. We were free to subscribe to the *New York Times* and have it delivered directly to our lawns each morning.

The Office of Price Administration terminated Los Alamos's set pricing. Fruits and vegetables were still limp, milk was still nearly sour when we got it, except now everything was nearly double the price.

A letter was sent out to us, addressed, *To all the women of Los Alamos*, and it requested we attend a meeting to help spread the facts about atomic bombs and dispel rumors. The meeting was led by Joan Hinton, the female scientist many of us disapproved of. We heard she had become increasingly critical of the bomb. In the gymnasium she held up what looked like a thin piece of flat glass and said, *Do you know what this is?* And we called out, *Glass!* And she said, *No, it is not glass. This is what an atom bomb does to the ground.*

She said, *We need to do something about this*, and she said, *We must send this glass to the mayors of every single major city in the United States*, and she said, *This could be all that is left of your hometown.* And we nodded as expected even if we did not like Joan and we politely declined to participate in anything she wanted. Or we volunteered and wrote letters to several mayors and asked them, *Do you want this to happen to your city?*

On the *New York Times* Sunday front page was an image of the city grid overlaid with an illustration of what might happen if a bomb were dropped in the middle of Manhattan: the rubble of music halls, hotels, art museums, galleries, all of that cultural history. Like Hiroshima, perhaps all that would be left of Manhattan Island would be one sturdy bank made from marble and reinforced for earthquakes. It would be as flat as Kansas, an urban prairie with views of the water. We had thought the Gadget would bring relief, but as soon as the bomb was used there was a new fear: if we could detonate it, so, too, could any enemy.

One night we found our husbands, or someone else's husband, sitting in the middle of the children's sandbox, still wearing work boots, and holding a rifle. *Bill?* we asked him from where we stood on the other side of the yard, but he disregarded our call or did not hear us. The sun was low behind the mountains and his back was to us — a blue-checkered shirt, we remember. *Bill,* we called again. He pointed the rifle to the sky. He pulled the trigger. The sound echoed, scattered a few starlings from the trees, and we shrieked. When we regained our wits we queried, *What on earth were you doing?* To which he replied, *I just needed to do something,* and got up from the sandbox. We turned and went back into the house.

Migraine medicine was still out of stock. A husband was injured at the Tech Area. His arms blistered, it spread up his body, the tissue died, and twenty-four days later he was dead. We asked, *How did this happen?* but we were not told.

One morning a husband from across the street called our name. We were out watering the flowers before anyone could see us using up water on such a luxury as a potted plant. With his arm he motioned for us to come over, and so we did, and once we got inside his house he raised his arm to our faces and we saw a welt across his forearm about four inches long. Did he smell like whiskey? We had never seen this man unreasonably distraught, or emotional much at all.

He went to his bedroom and pulled the covers up above his head. We asked, *What happened?* but he did not answer us. Around the room was a black burn mark up the wall from the oil heater, and it appeared as if it had malfunctioned, and burned his arm. What was a woman to do in this situation? Though we wanted to comfort him, we certainly did not want to find ourselves in another woman's bed. We assured him everything would be okay, and then we said that we would be right back, and hurried home, and sent our son or daughter to the commissary to find his wife, and to notify a doctor.

We saw our men sob into their pillows. But when we went by the military service club we saw GIs dancing and singing *When Johnny Comes Marching Home.*

Since the censorship was lifted, we could see our families for the first time in years, and we begged our parents to visit: *We think it would be tons of fun! Please think seriously about coming.* But we did not sound positive enough, and our fathers said they could not get away from the department store, the bank, the lab, or the university, but our mothers wrote and said they would come by train or bus as quickly as they could.

Our mothers came and though the altitude left them short of breath they were delighted that our children could speak since they had last seen them, or that there were more of them than before. They were surprised that the commissary carried mayonnaise and Kleenex, and they were pleased to see that we were not starving, and they were thrilled that our friends began calling them Mom, too.

We said it was like going to a funeral, watching everyone leave. The construction workers and machinists left first, gathering up their families and departing in a procession of trailers. For three years we had not ironed the good tablecloths, brought out the fine china, or asked, *Do you prefer white or red?* about the wine. Soon we would be away from one another and in other towns we would befriend the university president's wife by inviting her over for tea, and we would not be wearing blue jeans in her company. But we felt middle-aged at twenty-seven, and we would be thrilled to return to academic life afterward, if only because we would no longer be one of the oldest women in the room.

Before we left we went to the Army office and when it was our turn we gave our claim tickets to a man in order to retrieve our cameras from the Army vault. Instead we were told they could not be found. We were called Lady then, as in *Look, Lady, I have no way of finding them*, and he told us to pick out any camera we preferred.

We found a better camera for ourselves. Or we felt bad about taking someone else's things, and we could not find our own, and we returned home empty-handed. We brought back from those years very few pictures of that time, if any, and had no images of our children at three, at five, at seven, aside from those in our memories.

We went to Albuquerque or Santa Fe to celebrate our nearing and permanent departure as well as to buy university-appropriate attire to get our husbands ready for interviewing again. Our husbands said they could take academic jobs and we would starve or they could take industry jobs and we would eat well. Some of us encouraged our husbands to give up academia, saying, *I'm tired of rationing*, and some of us encouraged our husbands to give up physics entirely, saying, *You do not want to spend your entire life figuring out how to kill people, do you?* And some of us said, *You'll make the right choice.*

While we had spent three years in Los Alamos, our husbands had been promoted to full professors and the dean of the university wrote to say our husbands would now have their own research lab. Or while we were away many more schools were hiring — they anticipated GIs returning home and entering college — and our husbands had accomplished something, and on the Hill they had made friends with scientists from several universities, and they were offered better-paying jobs, with higher ranks, at more prestigious places, in larger cities. Though the Director was stepping down to return to his lab at Berkeley, the General invited himself to dinner at our place and suggested our husbands seriously consider the financial rewards a position at the Los Alamos Scientific Laboratory could offer our family. *Think of the stability.* Some of our husbands did just that and signed up for another year at Los Alamos despite our protests.

Our husbands went to cities to interview for jobs, and when they returned we discussed the options: an assistant professorship in New York or a job here at Los Alamos. Many of us had a bit of negotiating power since we'd been here so long and we protested, *That's three thousand miles away from Portland!* Or, *That's two thousand miles away from Kansas City!*

For a while many of us were ravenous for news and thought that the more information we had, the better chance there was of making a smart decision. But that faded for some of us, and we finally said, *Oh, to hell with it*, and moved to the city, or the coast. Besides, we could have a heart attack, get hit by a car, choke on a ham bone. What we learned was this: there were no ways to control unknown threats.

Our husbands considered staying. We thought the town would remain a military post, or that our husbands would be forced to leave their academic positions to conduct war research whenever the military so desired. Many of our husbands said they did not want to sell their souls and many of our husbands said, *I have to help see this thing through.* Some husbands could not make up their mind if it was right or wrong for science to serve war. Some said they preferred to teach and do research without the restrictions of secrecy.

One husband who deliberated about that question went on to build something bigger than the atomic bomb, the hydrogen bomb. We were slightly relieved to learn the Lab would no longer be under military control but transferred to a civilian agency, what became the Atomic Energy Commission. To stop the use of atomic bombs, some of our husbands worked on international agreements to outlaw the future development of atomic bombs. Or our husbands signed letters in support of military governance over atomic labs. They were our husbands and we thought what they thought, and we thought the opposite, and we tried to keep quiet, or we tried to be loud and have our voices heard.

Before we left we gave our old washing machine to Juanita, remembering when we did how scared she was the first time she used it; we sold our desk and thought of the nights we spent writing letters to our parents without saying anything specific; we sold our children's beds; we took our typewriters. That last week men came and installed a phone in our home for the new residents. We used it once to telephone the plumber.

GOING BACK

We were going back to Berkeley, New York, or Madison. We were going to Hiroshima. We were going to Oak Ridge. Three years in the desert and we were near thirty or past it. Our pants were thin, our shirts needed to be mended, and we had little idea what women wore these days. If we began as foreigners we became naturalized during these years and so we were not going back to France, Germany, or Italy. Some of us were staying, even after our husbands had promised this move was only temporary, and we were going back to a real city only in our imagination. Saying good-bye to our friends was not just saying good-bye to *them*, we were saying good-bye to a part of ourselves.

For those of us who were leaving, we thought for the first time we might miss Los Alamos. The piñons, the snowy vistas, the thin fresh air, the hard rain falling. On our last ride on the horses, Genevieve, who was returning to Britain, stopped, closed her eyes, and said, *All my life I will remember this sunshine.* We loved the hush the snow placed on the landscape, and we thought of the hand of God, or we thought of light, and we thought of the stillness of snow, how it quieted even our children. It was the earth winning a small battle.

Near the end we began to pull away from one another, we stopped by unannounced less frequently and started looking for the next thing. But we still threw parties. We hosted goodbye dinners that ended with *Auld Lang Syne* and tears. Some children ran around gathering autographs.

By the end of our time at Los Alamos we had two or ten black-on-black pieces of pottery and we wanted more. We wore weighty belts of silver. We bought high-topped deerskin moccasins. We spread Navajo rugs on our floor and draped Chimayo blankets over our couch. We decided we would like to live without gas and the daily newspaper. We decided we wanted to buy land like the Spanish and the Indians had, or we offered to buy what they owned.

We said so long with fruitcake, with lingering hugs, with quick pats on the back, with picnics at Frijoles Canyon. We took last rides on the horses. Katherine fell down a canyon wall and broke her neck and left Los Alamos in an off-white brace that constricted our ability to hold tightly to her. It was in the departure that we learned our true feelings: we would miss one another terribly.

The people of the San Ildefonso pueblo threw us a party. They fed us things they knew we liked — Jell-O and Coke. We called it a fiesta hoedown and brought hotdogs. The pueblo wives were encouraged by Po, the one Indian we had invited to our square dance group, to make authentic recipes. We ate prune pies that tasted like pemmican cakes; we ate tamales, tiny chicken rolls, tortillas, and squash mixtures. We ate things we could never figure out, but it all was delicious, and our hosts seemed to be enjoying the food as much as we were. There were pitchers of fruit juice and plenty of coffee. We begged for recipes.

We danced with the men we haggled with over bowls the week before. Or we attended out of obligation. Or we did not attend at all. Initially only the dance group members were invited, with a few exceptions made for the other women Louise liked: Dorothy, Edith, and Helen. But every woman had to promise they wouldn't tell anyone about the event. They promised, though everyone found out about it. Maria insisted on no alcohol, and Louise assured her, but given the rowdiness of the crowds, we thought that would be difficult.

The festivities opened with drums and a chanting chorus of men led by Montoya, our janitor from the Lodge. Po called us in for a square dance demonstration; we formed squares and designated Starla as the caller — we had long ago concluded that Starla's secret was that there was no secret. Our brief demonstration was followed by a group of Indian men with Cokes in their hands, shaking their bodies in motions we were nervous that we could not reproduce. Po called out in Tewa, and the group moved serpent-like. The governor of the pueblo, wearing a blue-and-white-checkered blanket over his shoulders, made gyrations we tried to follow. He put both hands on his head, as if they were antlers, and grinned. Some of us chuckled to see his missing two front teeth — but his feet kept perfect time. The intricate steps changed to another quite sophisticated move, and we followed as best we could. The drummers went faster and faster: it was a test of endurance we were sure to fail; we dared not stop. Montoya stood on a chair and shouted, above the fast drumbeat and shuffles: *This is the Atomic Age — This is the Atomic Age!*

BY THE END

A ceremony was to be held in Fuller Lodge to, as the announcement said, *acknowledge the scientific achievements of Los Alamos*. A stage was constructed and behind it a long banner of red, white, and blue. The President of the University of California came because the University of California partially ran Los Alamos, someone said, or since the Director taught there, perhaps, another person added, but the reason was unclear. The President stood in the middle of the stage wearing a double-breasted pinstriped suit and to his left the General wore his customary khaki, customarily wrinkled. To the right was the Director, who somehow seemed alone — he stared out into the crowd rather than speaking with the others on the stage and though he looked out at us, it was as if he looked out at nothing — his face was expressionless, which, given that it was an occasion of celebration, was in itself memorable. There were folding chairs for us to sit on, real chairs with backs instead of the hay bales we sat on to watch movies, and one wife in the crowd said, *Real chairs in the Lodge!*

We've made it now, and those around her chuckled.

Though there was a military band at every event, there wasn't this time, but four band members marched to the front of the stage, saluted the President, marched to the back of the Lodge, and sat down. The President walked to the microphone. He spoke about *the great achievements accomplished* and some of us noticed the Director's lack of attention. After polite claps for the President, the Director walked to the podium. It was his turn to thank the President, on behalf of all at Los Alamos, for the honor of this recognition. We leaned forward.

He thanked the President. He thanked us. He repeated his previous words of caution. He sat down.

When it was the General's turn to speak he did not contradict the Director but gave further cautions: *We are at a crossroads between annihilation and peace. My hope is that the world leaders will work together to ensure safety for us all.* And with that he was not the frumpy man who loved his chocolate and controlled our whereabouts, but a reasonable person who expressed the gravity of the circumstances.

He was our General then, just as the Director had always been our Director. Here we were, together, on the brink of a future we could not predict — more unknowns were yet to come — but we were very aware of it. We clapped, we stood and clapped, we hooted, we cried, we hugged. And with that, our war and our duty here at Los Alamos were, for many of us, officially, over.

OUR LAST

Our husbands came home from the Tech
Area for the last time and invited us to be
their guests at Chez Mess Hall. We said, *What
a fancy place! Are you sure we can afford it?*
Or, *I'll have to curl my hair first.* We stepped
into the warm crowd of the mess hall, stood
behind GIs and other families, and picked up
a thin metal tray dented around the edges
from use. It was our last dinner. Down the
line we walked, greeting San Ildefonso
men and women or WACs who scooped hot
meat, green beans, rehydrated potatoes, and
ash-colored gravy into each of the four compartments on our metal tray. The narrow
compartments made our more soupy items
swim into other things: a slight tilt of the tray
or our hand and we were soon eating ice
cream topped with pork gravy. And to think
some people — the GIs, the single men
— put up with this meal three times a day for
three years.

In line behind us was our obstetrician, Dr.
Kashavarez, and his family, and in front of us
was Margaret, who was five months pregnant

and who had been chastised earlier that day by Dr. K for gaining twenty-five pounds. His wife was a rail, her eyes gaunt, set far back, with dark semicircles beneath them. Margaret declined the potatoes and we continued down the line, both gazing longingly at the sundaes. One of us said, *We lost our baby weight last time so who cares?* It was our last day here and after tomorrow we'd never see Dr. K again. We let the hot fudge drop long and slow atop our vanilla scoops but avoided eye contact with him through dinner.

The days became caravans of departing Studebakers and Cadillacs. Some of us were going back to England. Or we were staying in New Mexico and buying abandoned cattle ranches, or haciendas, or fishing cabins. A few of us were staying, unfortunately, in our plain green houses. We were designing Western homes made of stone, or adobe, or logs. We were planning brick homes in the Midwest with concrete frames and finished basements.

And we felt the deflation that comes when one gets what one has wanted: it was not quite what it seemed it would be. We thought of the time when we first arrived, when only a stack of pine boards were all that existed of the houses, when garbage cans overflowed.

How dust rose in great clouds beyond the set of older buildings. How we arrived and thought it was not beautiful, though we complimented the mountains to one another.

We left with more children than we came with and less wedding china. We left with black bowls, bright rugs, needles, thread, and muddy boots on our feet. We looked back on the time of our arrival to Los Alamos, how we felt very young. Some of us thought it was much better then, earlier, before we understood anything, though in our futures there was much more to learn.

And if we wanted a sentimental good-bye, instead of going directly down the Hill to Santa Fe we drove past Valle Grande — the crater of a volcano, the high mountain roads, the rare dark clouds gathering and the wildflowers blooming in the caldera.

THE DIRECTOR

We left and the Director would be taken to trial on accusations of disloyalty. Though he was trusted to orchestrate the creation of the atomic bomb, he was now deemed a security risk. Had he consorted with Communists? Was he a spy? We were asked to speak against him and we refused, as did our husbands.

The Director did not encourage the creation of a hydrogen bomb, something even more destructive than the atomic bomb. He doubted it was feasible and said it would be too destructive to use in war, even if it would be, he said, *technically sweet*. Helen's husband wanted to make this bomb and he wanted to be in charge of it. Her husband spoke against the former Director and told the Senate Committee: *One would be wiser not to grant security clearance to Oppenheimer.* We thought her husband was bitter for not being chosen for the lab leader way back when, and many of us, including our husbands, said if they were ever alone with him they would give him what for.

We felt bad for Helen — who somehow had to put up with the bravado, late night piano playing, and ignorance of him. To be the wife of a man that spoke out against the Director, who worked to get the Director's security clearance revoked, to be the wife of the man who became the father of the super-bomb. Her husband was on record, in court, saying: *In a great number of cases I have seen Dr. Oppenheimer act — I understood that Dr. Oppenheimer acted — in a way which for me was exceedingly hard to understand. I would personally feel more secure if public matters would rest in other hands.*

And because all of Oppenheimer's business was in the news and for many years he was followed by the FBI, we learned that while he was Director, and married to Kitty, he had flown to California and stayed the night at his former girlfriend's home. She was a psychologist, a colleague's daughter, and a Communist. Soon after his visit, she was found dead, and the death was considered a suicide. Her last note said: *I wanted to live, but I got paralyzed somehow.* This was fascinating and horrifying information, and some of us were not surprised, but what did it all mean?

The Director's security clearance was revoked by the Atomic Energy Commission in 1954 and his office at the White House was terminated. But nine years later, he was given a $50,000 award by the Atomic Energy Commission, an award named after one of our husbands, for *his outstanding contributions to theoretical physics and his scientific and administrative leadership*. He died, before many, but not all, of our husbands, from cancer, in 1967. The trouble with Oppenheimer, the famous but uninvolved scientist Einstein remarked, was that he loved a woman who did not love him back: the U.S. government.

OUR CHILDREN

Our children left Los Alamos thinking they were a part of something important, and they adopted the language of their fathers and us, or the opposite. They said, during high school debates, *It needed to be done! Or, We had no choice! Or, They would have surrendered if we just told them what we could do.*

Some of our children saved cereal box tops and sent away for atomic bomb rings. They received a plastic ring with a secret compartment so that they could *look at flashes caused by atoms splitting like crazy in the sealed warhead chamber.* By this time, some of our children had seen the real thing by watching tests in Nevada, and this ring seemed quite inexact. Our daughters wore two-piece bathing suits called bikinis, after Bikini Island, one of the Marshall Islands where several nuclear explosions cratered and irradiated land and sea.

We left and our Davids and Emilys and Marys and Michaels went to college. Our Bills grew their hair past their shoulders. And

248

they came home and said they would not eat food in our house because it was the *fruits of war*. They said they were purging themselves through anti-nuclear-proliferation protests. We said, *Don't be silly, Mary,* and we said, *For heaven's sakes, Michael!* but some of us understood their feelings, and some of us said nothing.

Our children accused us of only caring about money; they said we forgot about how the rest of the world struggled because we no longer struggled ourselves, if we ever did. They blamed us for New Mexico's economic reliance on the nuclear industry. They asked their fathers, *Don't you feel guilty? How could you go through with it?* And we cringed and we knew what they meant and we wondered that ourselves, or we felt angry and protective and we said, *Don't speak like that to your father.* Our husbands answered, saying, *No, I don't feel guilty. It needed to be done. If it wasn't them it would've been us.* Or they said, *Yes,* and quoted the Director: *The deep things in science are not found because they are useful, they are found because it was possible to find them.*

We pondered what it would be like to be our daughters, to be living as a woman in another generation, and we felt a bit jealous. We thought our daughters had many more freedoms than we did in choosing a career — they did not have to be schoolteachers or secretaries — in traveling alone — they could just pick up and move across the country — in taking oneself to a movie in the middle of a Sunday afternoon. Or we could see how so many options might render decisions more difficult to make. And when they said, *The only way to improve the world is to protest war*, we thought them unreasonably idealistic, or we thought them more of what the world needed.

Our children said they would go to jail rather than be drafted. And some of us worried we had spoiled them somehow. Our children said they did not tell their friends what their fathers did because their fathers worked for *the man*, but we thought that keeping quiet about Los Alamos and the violence or triumph of what our husbands did was not because they felt a sense of responsibility to a collective; rather, they felt the shame of the individual: they were worried about their own reputations. Or all that secret keeping had deeply affected them. The outside world seemed very nosy.

Perhaps some of our children did care about their country in the ways some of us understood, and they volunteered for the Vietnam War rather than protesting it, and they came back changed, as we knew they would, though the particulars of those changes were mysterious. Edward was much more tidy and pensive after his return, and married Anne, who worked as a cashier at Dot's Market and brought us embroidered napkins. They went on to have four children, and experience the shifts and swings of marriages, but nothing too serious. David appeared more cynical, went back to school to study philosophy, and called himself a poet. Tim moved back in with us, nailed quilts to his bedroom wall to cover the windows, slept during the day, and woke with nightmares. Bobby married, though his wife appeared more and more tired over the years, and he brought a twelve-pack to every family gathering, even Sunday brunch, and we sensed something was not right, but any interference was met with anger. Our children carried concealed weapons, had gun collections, refused to sit with their backs to any window. Or they came home from Vietnam and they were quiet about their time there and we could not tell what effect the war had on them at all, except they seemed more grateful for our macaroni loaf.

They had known war differently than us and our husbands. They had seen death more immediately: the eyes of people whom we called our enemy.

Some of us did not mind that our children no longer went to church or synagogue, some of us thought the fact that our children were gay might make life complicated, or maybe not, and we accepted that our children supported abortion rights. When they brought home brownies they were the best brownies we had ever tasted and after two brownies we felt the tickling of the wind on our cheeks and we just wanted to watch the clouds pass overhead and tell our children how much we loved and admired them. We felt very calm, perhaps even happy.

Our children grew up; they became engineers, peace activists, grade school teachers, housewives, photographers, writers, bums. They became landscape painters, vice presidents of banks, psychologists; they became the children we outlived; they became the children who died of lung cancer; they became botanists, directors of physics labs, park rangers, geologists, lawyers, and environmental activists.

They finished college and did not see any reason to rush into getting a job or marrying and instead they sold all of their possessions and joined what they called a commune and what we called a cult.

Our children claimed to be conscientious objectors, they said they were going to *bum around Europe* with their girlfriends and boyfriends after college, and we objected, *You are ruining your life!* Or we thought they would not actually do it, so we just raised an eyebrow, but they did just that, they went.

And they were young and we thought they would grow out of it. Or we could see their point, but we did not know of alternatives, or we joined our children in protests. Or to really protest the war our children thought they needed to know more about history and so instead of sit-ins they went to graduate school. Some dropped out, got married, and went back to study biology. And no one was hiring in biology, but Los Alamos was hiring scientists for their computer skills, and we knew people, and our husbands knew people, and so our children moved back to Los Alamos and worked at the lab their fathers worked at, partly, they said, so their own three children could live as close to nature as they had, or to live close to us, their grandparents.

Our children did not directly work on bombs, but they built computer programs to assist with bomb making, and they said they felt conflicted, and they said, *If I had a perfect freedom of choice I wouldn't do it*, and they said, *I just have to put up with some stuff I'm not comfortable with in order to give my kids a good home*, and they said, *I have to sacrifice some of my conscience for some other benefits*.

They said they didn't really appreciate what their fathers did until they returned to the Lab to work there themselves. They said their work was of a secret nature but if atomic weapons were used on a new war over oil they would quit their jobs at Los Alamos, they really would.

Or our children went to the Marshall Islands as Peace Corps members because though the Marshallese had been evacuated from Bikini Island, they were moved to nearby islands, close enough to atomic testing to birth dead babies, or living babies that they called *jellyfish babies* for their half-formed limbs. Scientists wondered, *What are the effects of nuclear fallout on pregnant women and their fetuses?* Now there was evidence. Our children saw that a curtain had been drawn back.

Our children returned to New Mexico as they always thought they would and we went back to visit them. We went back and we saw a fast food restaurant erected where a lab once was. The guard gate was taken down. We saw many more concrete block lab buildings painted white.

While our children were at work we made tea in their sky-lighted houses, fetched the paper from the front steps, and read the *New Mexican Reporter* with interest. Some residents claimed there was a significant increase in brain cancer in one particular neighborhood close to the canyon, a beloved canyon of ours now disgraced with the nickname Acid Canyon, and some of us thought that was where materials had been dumped, and we did not know what to make of it. We heard that the golf course we had made was given a nice facelift, and that the social groups we started had grown by the hundreds, and we were delighted to be asked for an interview by the Los Alamos Historical Society. On a Friday afternoon we took the public bus,

Atomic City Transit, to that lodge we slept in the first day we arrived at Los Alamos in 1943.

On our bus ride we passed the visitor center, which was in a strip mall, and we stopped at the science museum. We read about the fused sand, the proliferation of honey pot ants as natural miners of the area; we saw photos of the female scientists enlarged and framed on the walls, images of these women then, during the war years, and now, on their front porches, without their husbands. *For goodness' sake*, we said, to no one in particular.

During our interview we were asked, *What was it like?* And we answered questions about what it was like then, and we felt a mix of emotions recalling that time: sadness for what was now in the past, but happiness about the recollection. We were pleased to visit the two museums in town and read our own family stories on the walls, to see a copy of a letter we wrote our mother in 1944, how Bobby was doing fine, how we really needed long johns. Inside one museum we saw Nancy's birth certificate framed with the birth location listed as Post Office Box 1663. And we thought of what was in the letter that we did not say, how we made our voices sound lighter than we felt when writing to our mothers.

Though no cameras were allowed at Los Alamos back when we arrived during the war, a few of us brought two cameras and only gave the Army one. And after the war we had these images developed — our children as toddlers, in a row of four, with their shirts off, splashing in the mud; our husbands standing at the top of a mesa with a walking stick they picked up on a hike, our husbands with their strong thighs and goofy smiles; and us, on the horses, our heads tilted back in laughter.

WE LEFT

Who we were before the war was still who we were during, and after. Somewhere inside we were still twenty-five, still feisty, emboldened, a riot.

But we were changed.

We left and lectured on atomic energy. We left and wrote autobiographies about life on the Hill. In our memoirs we reported that at Los Alamos there were no unemployed people, no in-laws, no invalids, no poor, and no sidewalks. Our memoirs suggested we knew nothing about what our husbands were building and we were accused of exaggerating how little we knew. But if other wives knew something, they did not tell those secrets to the rest of us, mostly.

We left and many things turned atomic: there was talk of nuclear power generators to replace coal and oil, and that we could sanitize our vegetables by irradiating them. Home furnishings became atomic, too — we bought clocks with rays and spheres showing the path of electrons around the nuclei of atoms.

We left and founded organizations that opposed nuclear weapons. We continued atomic research, we became social workers, we became grand-mothers, we became blacklisted. From an essay Robert published in the *Bulletin of Atomic Scientists* many years later we learned what had happened that Christmas Eve we saw him leaving in a rush: when it became clear that the Germans had abandoned their bomb project, and after overhearing the General say the bomb was being built to show Russia what the U.S. could do, Robert asked permission to leave and return to Britain. He became the only scientist to leave the project for reasons of conscience. Robert asked in his essay, as we also wondered: *Why did others not leave, too?*

Our husbands were curious. They wanted to know if their theoretical predictions could become a physical reality. They thought thou-sands of lives would be saved by a quick end to the war. Or perhaps they did not want to take a position because they feared how it might negatively affect their careers. Robert left and used his knowledge of physics to research the biological effects of radiation. He left and argued that all scientific research should be for the benefit for humanity, and that scientists cannot keep scientific curiosity and moral implications separate no matter how

difficult it might be to predict how such dis-
coveries might later be used.

Our husbands flew to the Marshall Islands
and we called them the Bikini scientists. A
navy official told Chief Juda, *We are testing
these bombs for the good of mankind, and to
end all world wars.* Juda understood the
word, *mankind*, from the Bible and replied, *If
it is in the name of God, I am willing to let
my people go.* Marshallese were told they
would be able to return after the bombs were
dropped but their homes, bicycles, and
bathtubs became radioactive. Though they
could not return, the radioactivity was fodder
for scientific research.

Meanwhile, we were featured in *Mademoi-
selle.* We went to work for the FBI. We wrote
textbooks, led high school physics programs,
became president of women's universities,
divorced. We made pineapple upside-down
cake for the first time in years.

We left and moved to places where air raid
sirens blared, where we dropped and covered,
where we feared someone else would use
what our husbands first developed on us and
we practiced drills to move our families
quickly into nuclear fallout shelters.

We left and said the Hill was an anthill and the bomb was its queen. But many of us told everyone, when we got back to civilian life, *There was no crime at all in Los Alamos. We all kept our doors unlocked. It was the safest place to raise a family.*

We left happy, we left relieved, we left thinking we had been a part of something unique, we left with doubts about our husbands, or about ourselves, or our country, or all of these, or none of it. We left wanting most what we had once had in the middle of the howling night, our friends: Louise, Starla, Margaret, Ingrid. We left pregnant, we left tired, we left, in some ways, just as we arrived: dusty and in need of a shampoo.

ACKNOWLEDGMENTS

Thank you to Julie Barer, who saw the project's heart and was essential in opening it up. Thank you to Nancy Miller, for your trust in the book and for those few, but exacting, suggestions. You two together, along with the teams of Barer Literary and Bloomsbury, have created the dream experience for a first book.

Thank you George Gibson, Alexandra Pringle, Helen Garnons-Williams, Summer Smith, Cristina Gilbert, Patti Ratchford, Lea Beresford, Nikki Baldauf, Elizabeth Van Itallie, and Emily DeHuff. Thank you William Boggess, Gemma Purdy, and Leah Heifferon. Thank you Heather McClenahan, Rebecca Collinsworth, and all of those involved with the Los Alamos Historical Society for honoring and archiving so many lives at Los Alamos. Thank you Jane Viste, who after a reading of mine probably most focused on the aesthetics of Cherenkov radiation, expressed interest in these scientists' wives and thus moved my attention.

Several books provide inspiration for this project, among them: Patrik Ouědník's

Europeana: A Brief History of the Twentieth Century, Juliana Spahr's *The Transformation*, Virginia Woolf's *Orlando*. More than several books compile a brief bibliography of Los Alamos or the period: Phyllis K. Fisher's *Los Alamos Experience*, Jane Wilson and Charlotte Serber's *Standing By and Making Do: Women of Wartime Los Alamos*, Eleanor Jette's *Inside Box 1663*, Bernice Brode's *Tales of Los Alamos: Life on the Mesa 1943–1945*, Leona Marshall Libby's *The Uranium People*, Laura Fermi's *Atoms in the Family*, Emily Yellin's *Our Mothers' War*, Studs Turkel's *The Good War*, Jennet Conant's *109 East Palace: Robert Oppenheimer and the Secret City of Los Alamos*, Jon Hunner's *Inventing Los Alamos: The Growth of an Atomic Community*, and Edith Warner's *In the Shadow of Los Alamos: Selected Writings*.

Thank you to my family, both here and gone. Thank you, Dr. Hall and the infinite empathy of the maternity ward night shift at Swedish.

Thank you to the late Elspeth Pope for seeing me fit for residency at Hypatia-in-the-Woods when I had just started this project, and thanks to the University of Washington in Tacoma for a Cascadia home. Thank you to the University of Denver and Washington University in St. Louis, for the time to write

263

and the community to write within.

Thank you to my teachers, who are my friends, and my friends, who are my teachers: Shena McAuliffe, Jesse McCaughey, Jen Denrow, Sara Witt, Yanara Friedland, Poupeh Missaghi, Joe Lennon, Sarah Vap and her Salish Sea Workshop, Todd Fredson, Eliana Schonberg, Rachel Sullivan Adams, Molly Langmuir, Cynda Collins Arsenault, Brigid McAuliffe, Mary Jo Bang, Kathryn Davis, Laird Hunt, Eleni Sikelianos, Selah Saterstrom, Adam Rovner, and Brian Kitely.

Thank you to my husband, Jerritt Collord.